JAZZ PIANO SOLOS   VOLUME 31

cocktail piano

Arranged by Brent Edstrom

ISBN 978-1-4803-6237-6

Visit Hal Leonard Online at
www.halleonard.com

Contact us:
Hal Leonard
7777 West Bluemound Road
Milwaukee, WI 53213
Email: info@halleonard.com

In Europe, contact:
Hal Leonard Europe Limited
42 Wigmore Street
Marylebone, London, W1U 2RN
Email: info@halleonardeurope.com

In Australia, contact:
Hal Leonard Australia Pty. Ltd.
4 Lentara Court
Cheltenham, Victoria, 3192 Australia
Email: info@halleonard.com.au

BLUE MOON

Music by RICHARD RODGERS
Lyrics by LORENZ HART

Slow, driving Swing

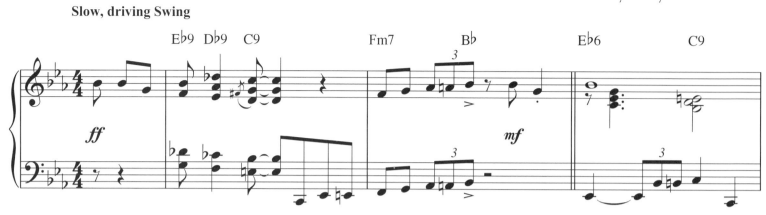

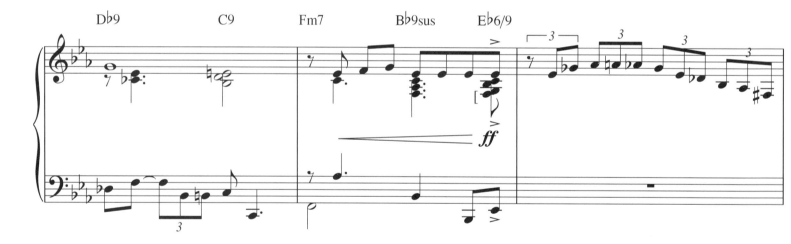

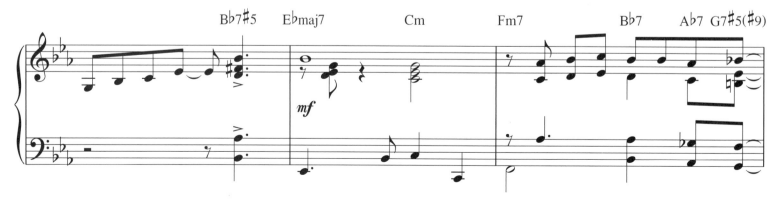

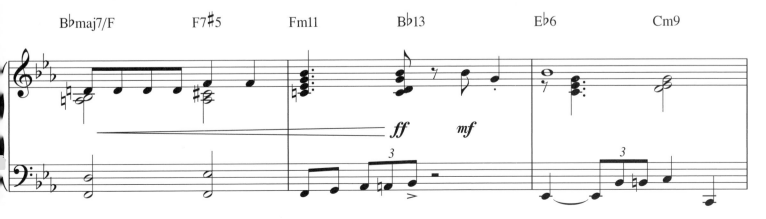

4

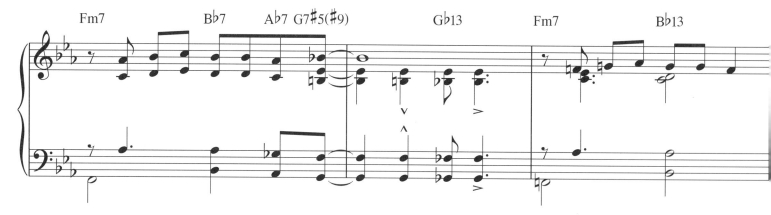

To Coda ⊕

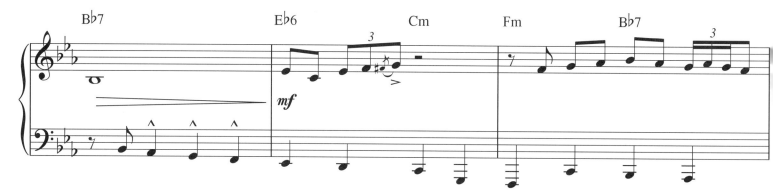

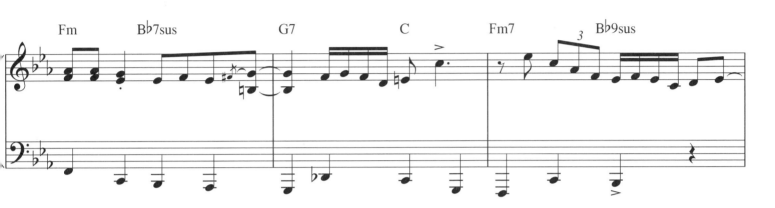

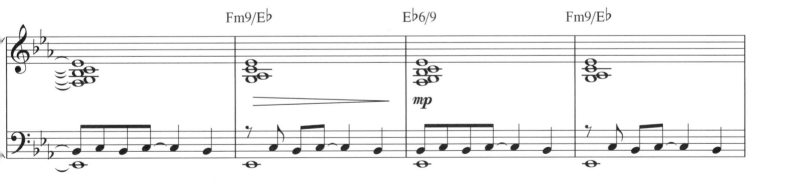

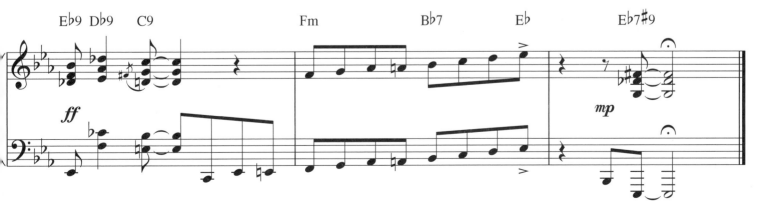

CHANGE PARTNERS
from the RKO Radio Motion Picture CAREFREE

Words and Music by
IRVING BERLIN

Moderate Bossa Nova

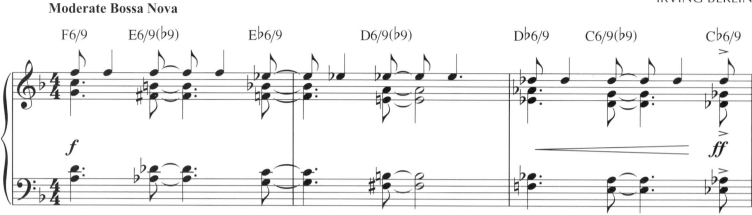

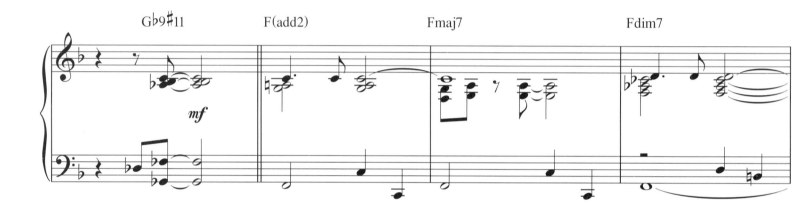

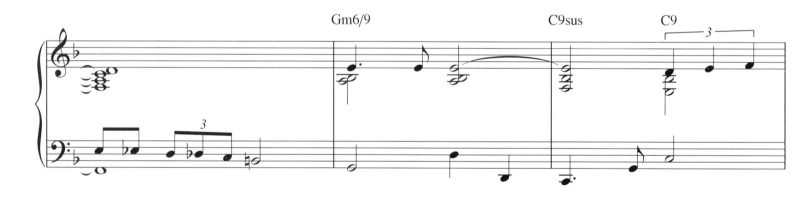

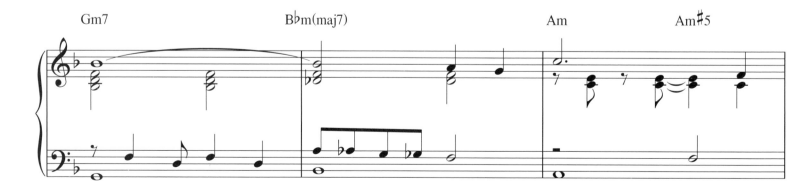

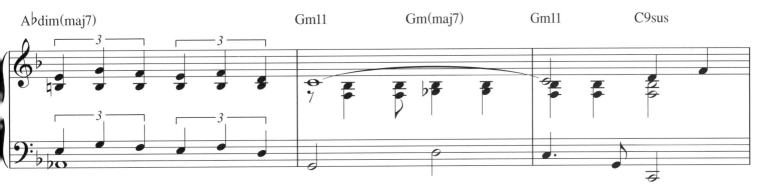

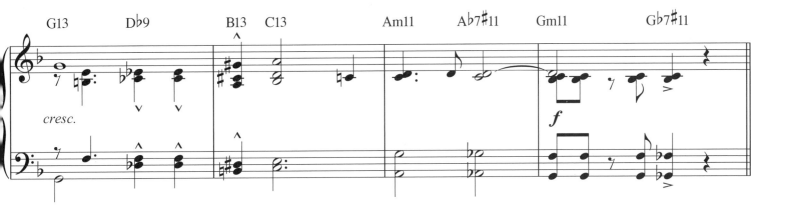

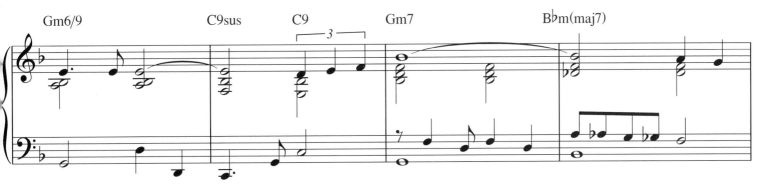

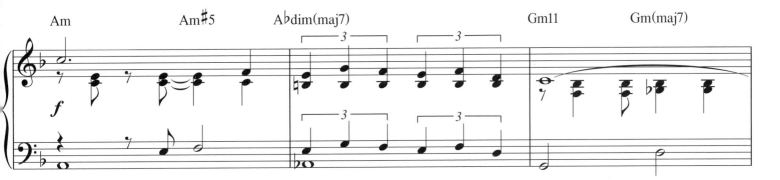

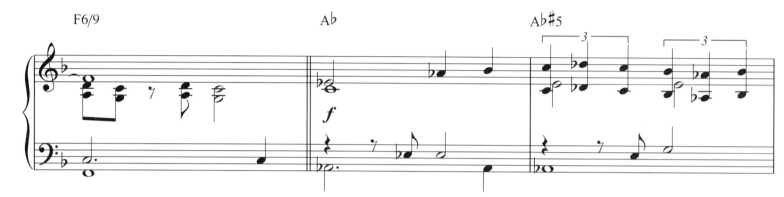

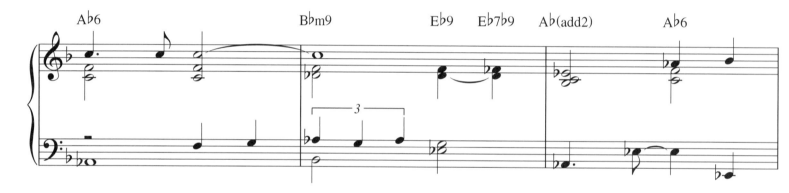

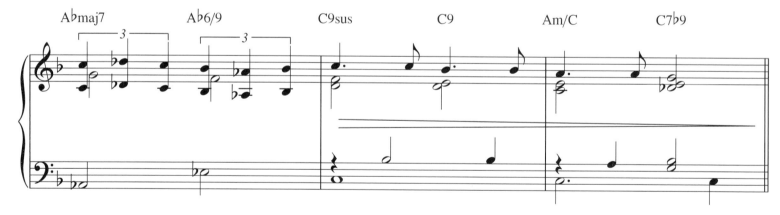

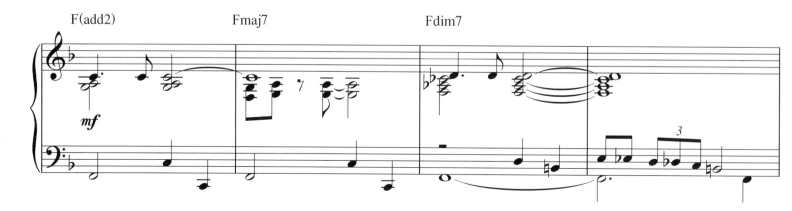

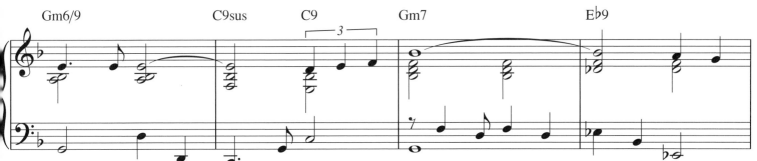

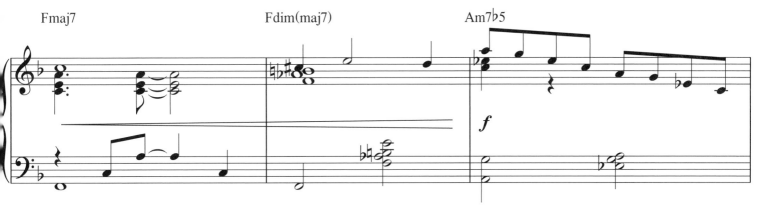

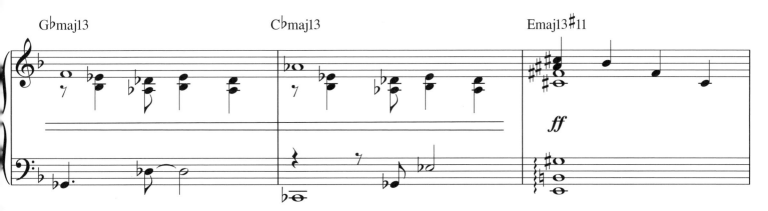

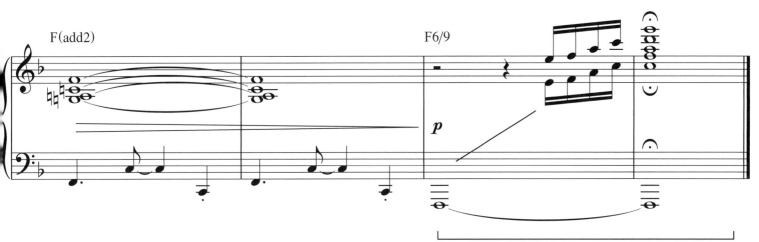

CHEEK TO CHEEK
from the RKO Radio Motion Picture TOP HAT

Words and Music by
IRVING BERLIN

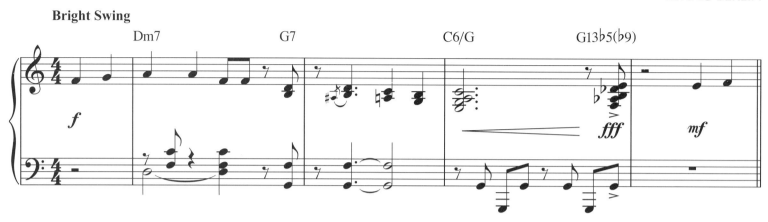

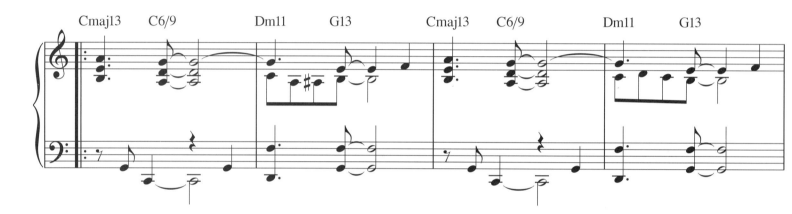

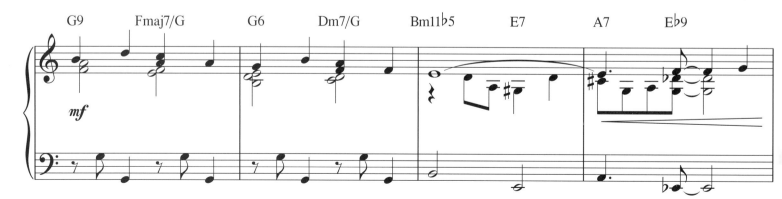

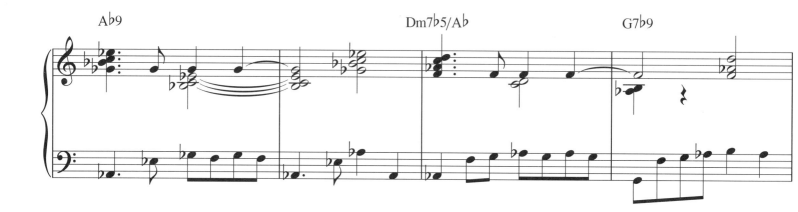

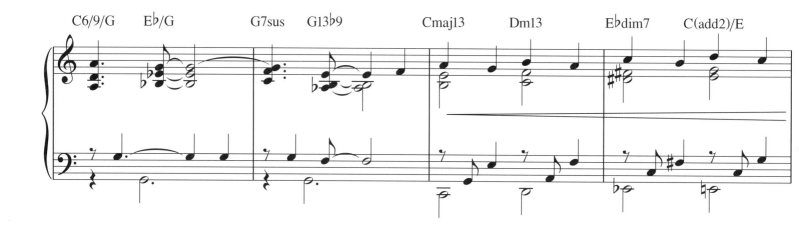

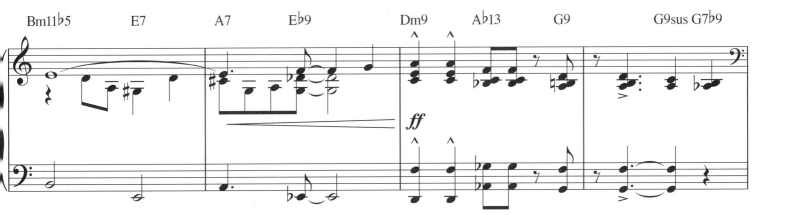

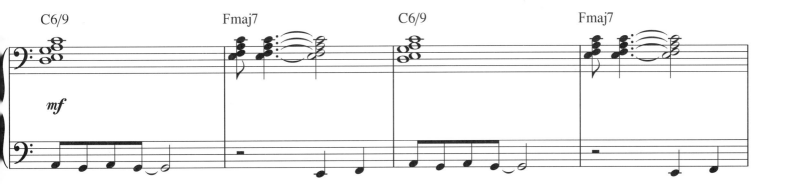

COCKTAILS FOR TWO
from the Paramount Picture MURDER AT THE VANITIES

Words and Music by ARTHUR JOHNSTON
and SAM COSLOW

Moderately, straight 8ths

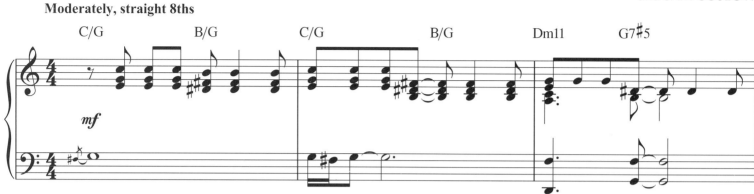

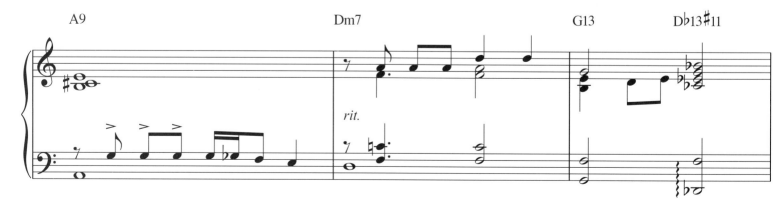

Moderate Swing

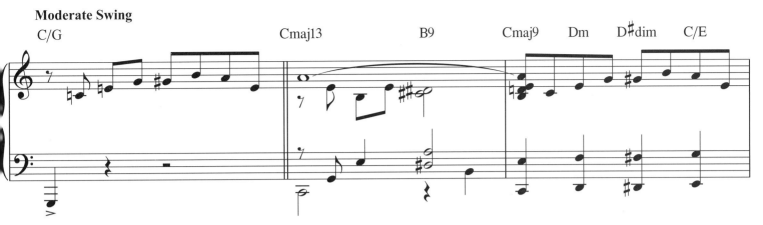

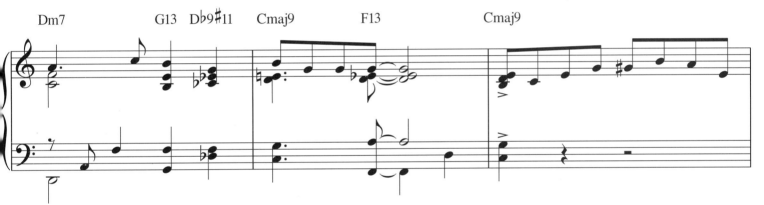

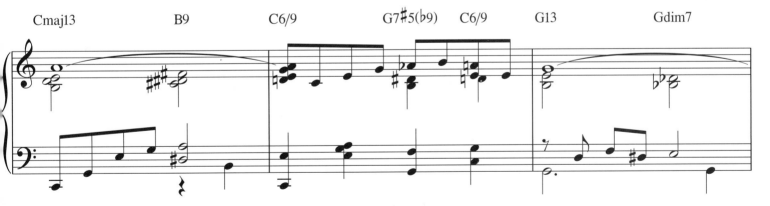

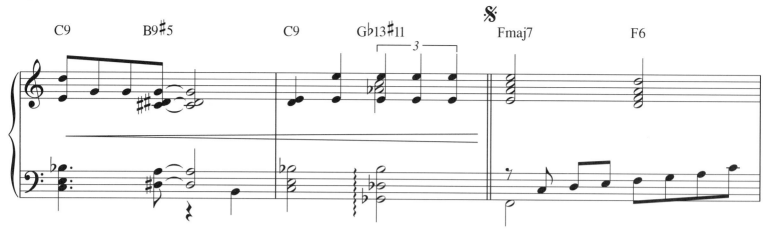

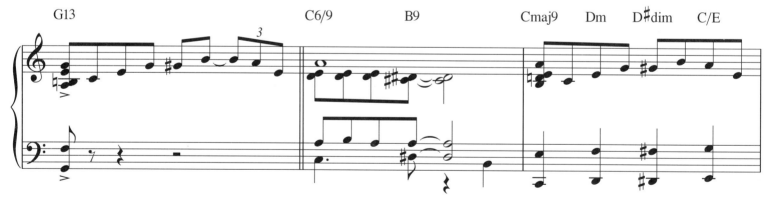

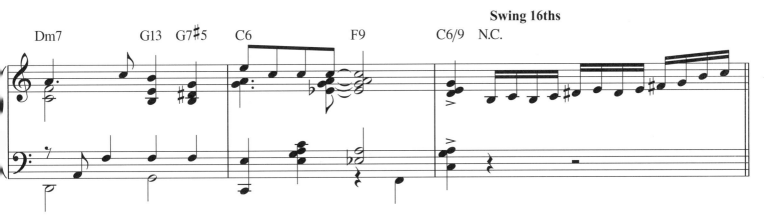

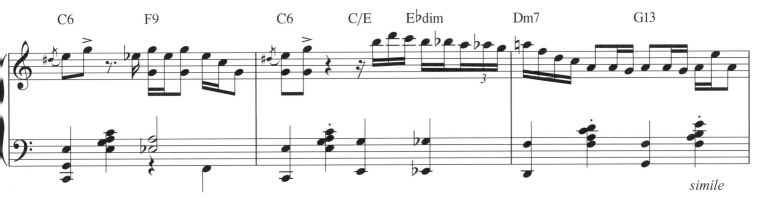

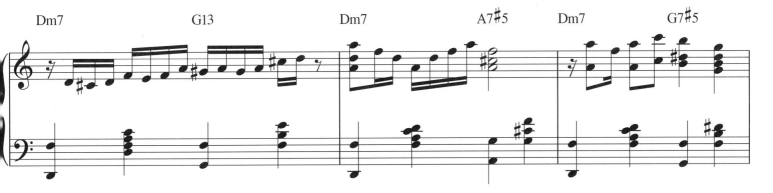

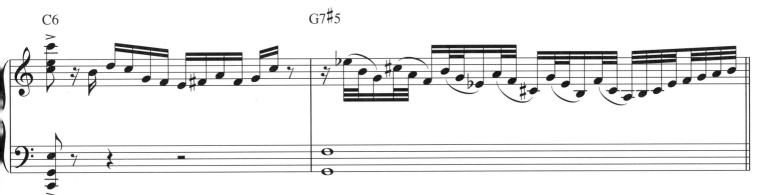

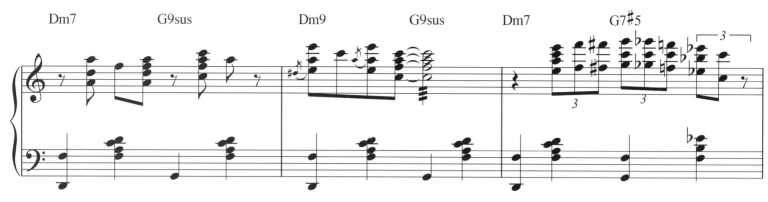

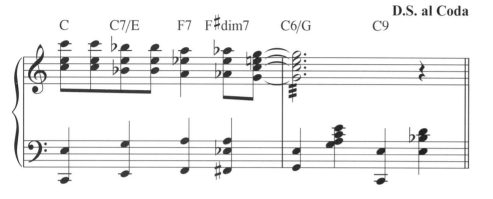

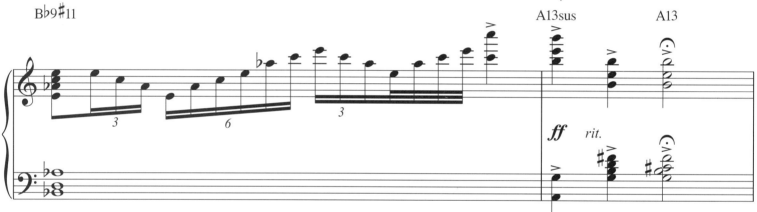

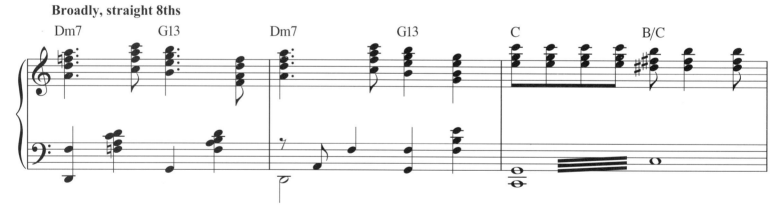

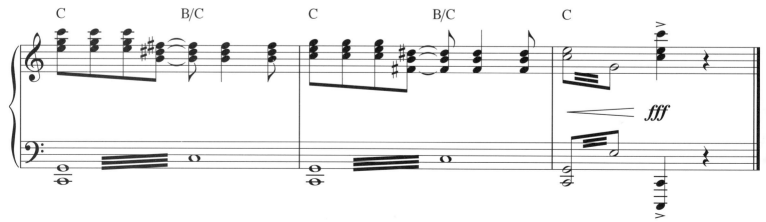

DREAM A LITTLE DREAM OF ME

Words by GUS KAHN
Music by WILBUR SCHWANDT
and FABIAN ANDREE

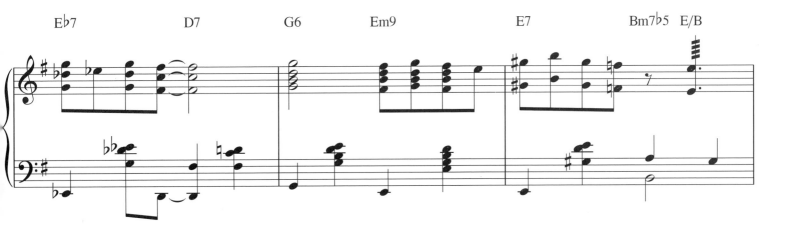

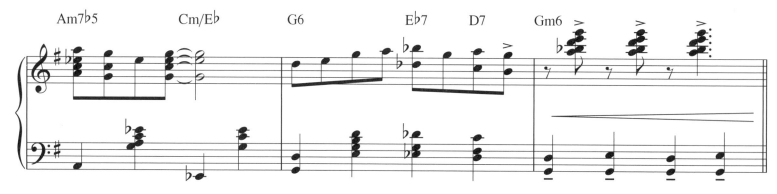

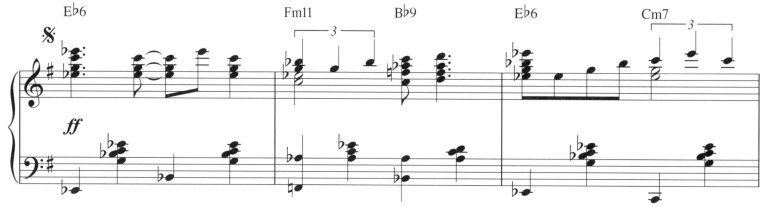

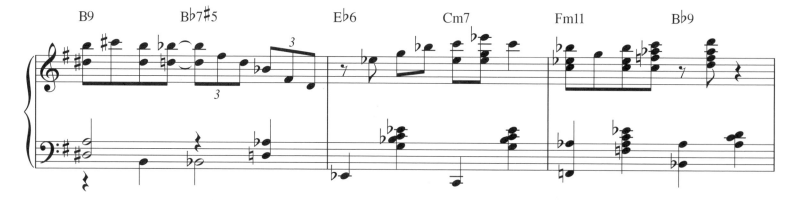

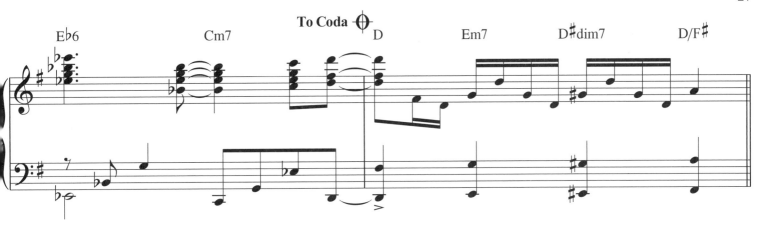

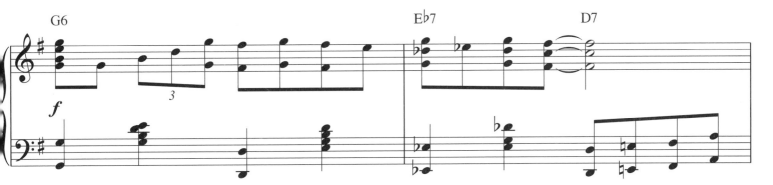

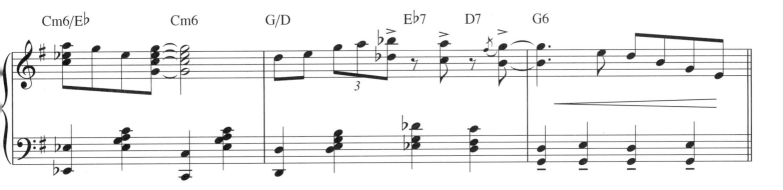

22

D.S. al Coda

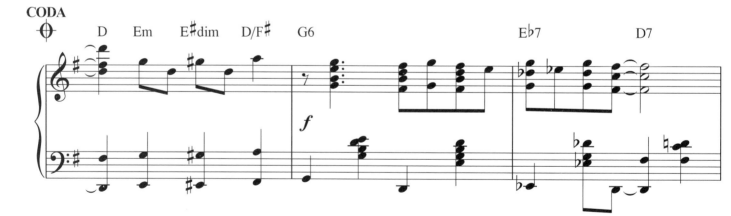

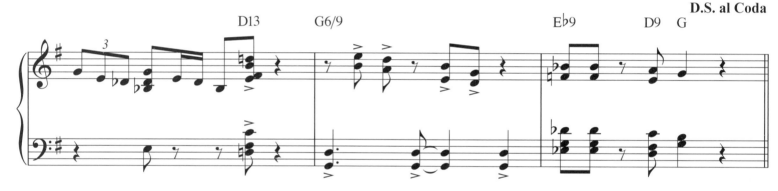

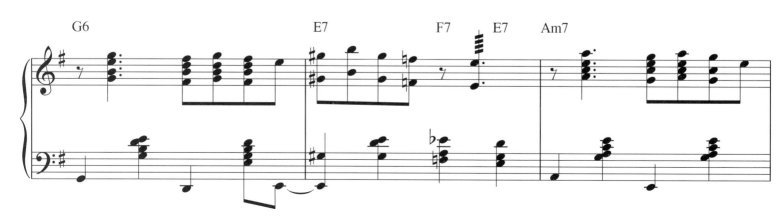

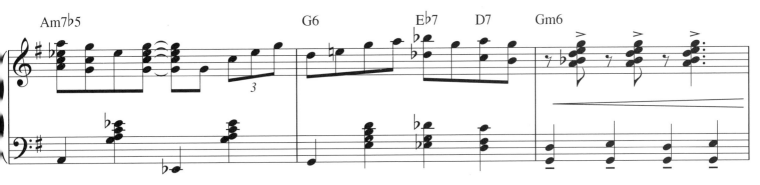

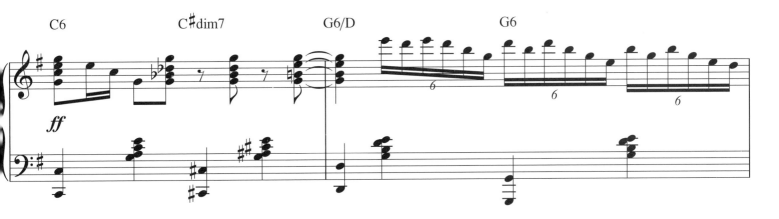

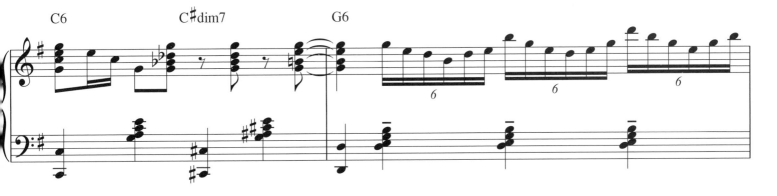

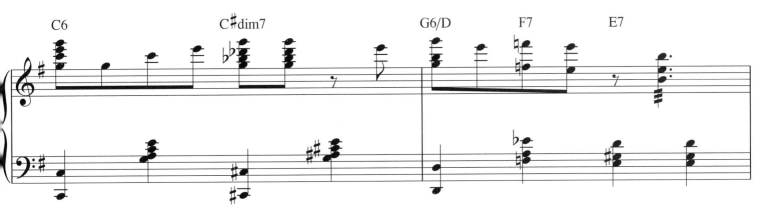

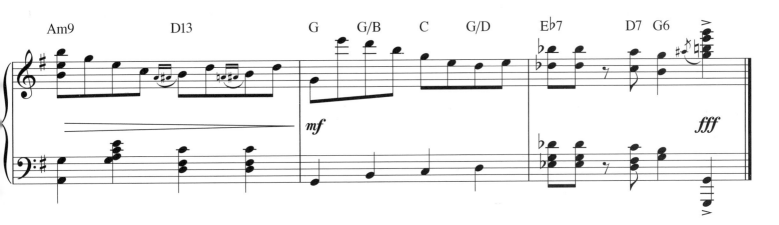

FLY ME TO THE MOON
(In Other Words)

Words and Music by
BART HOWARD

Moderate Swing

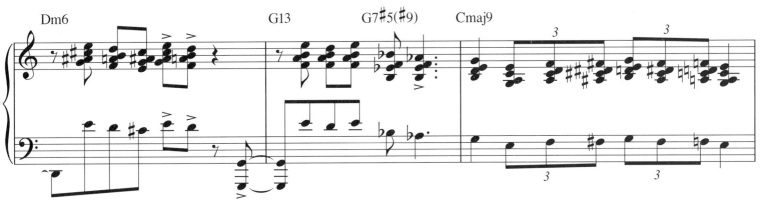

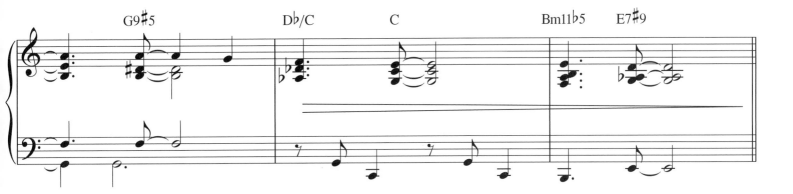

HEY THERE
from THE PAJAMA GAME

Words and Music by RICHARD ADLER
and JERRY ROSS

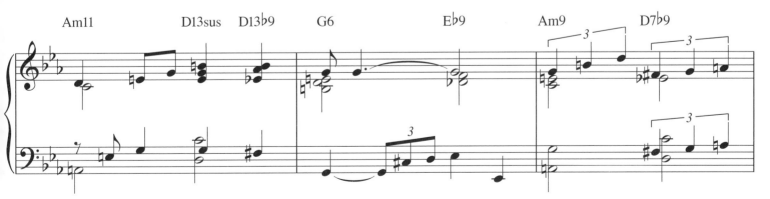

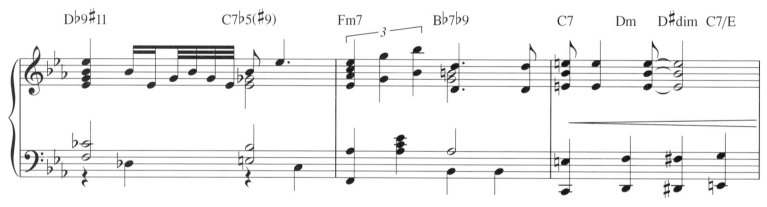

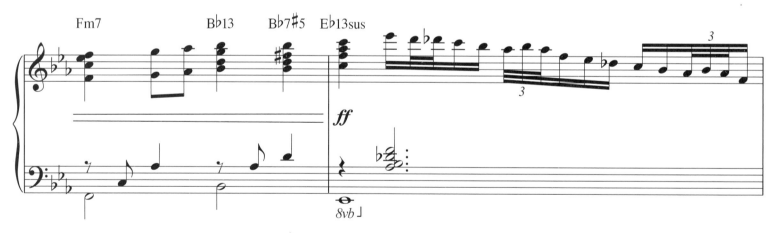

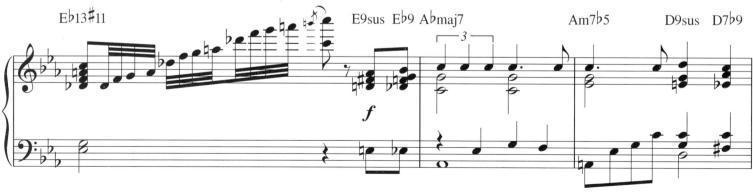

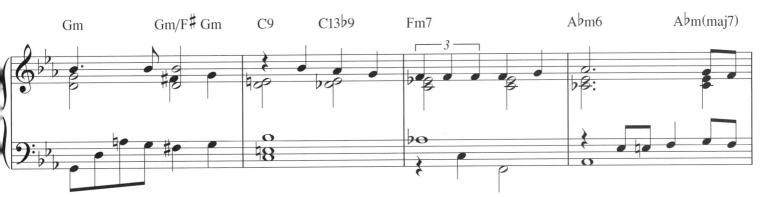

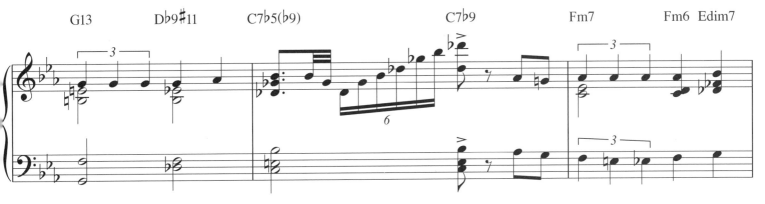

GEORGIA ON MY MIND

Words by STUART GORRELL
Music by HOAGY CARMICHAEL

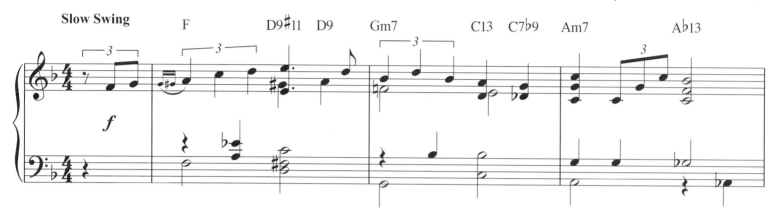

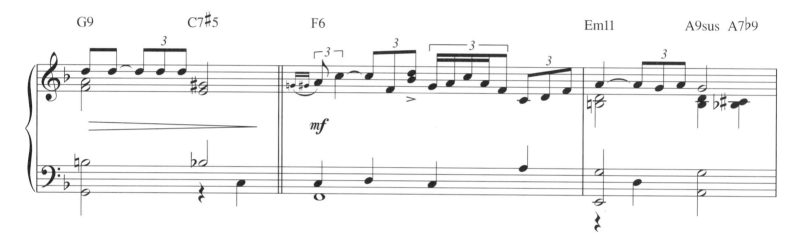

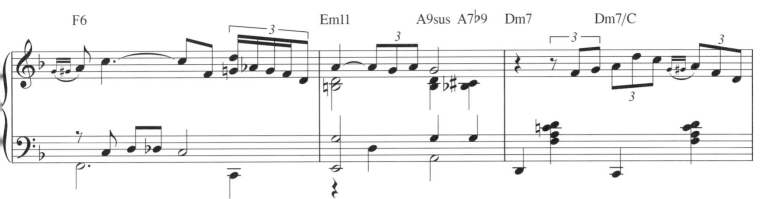

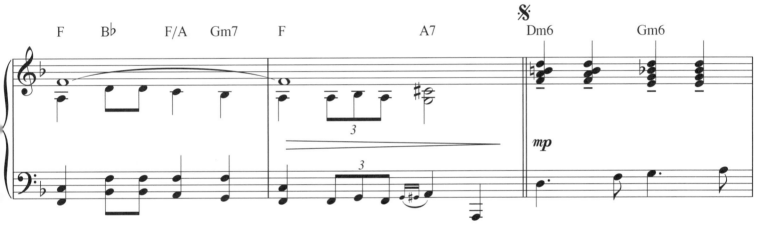

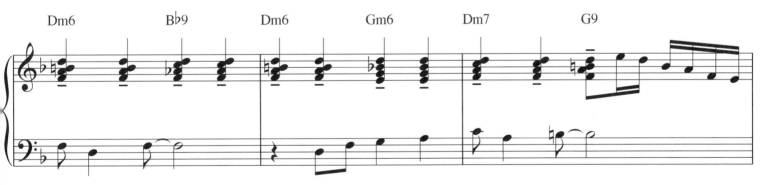

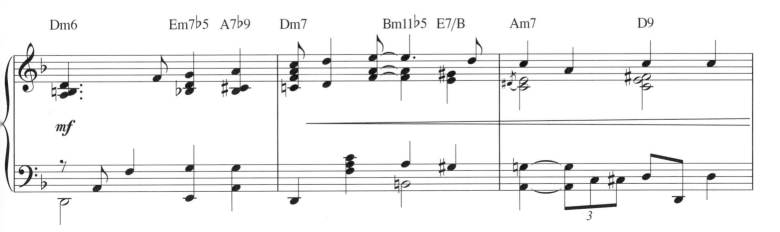

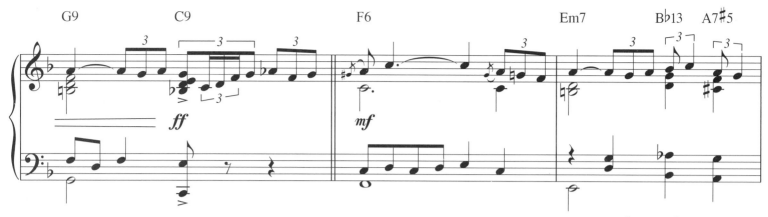

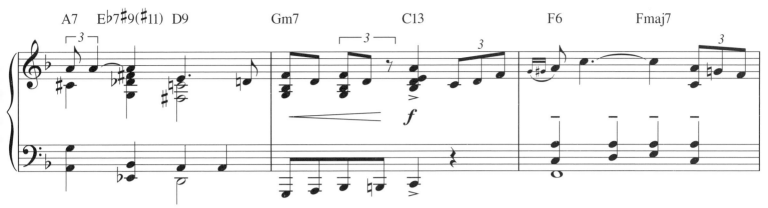

D.S. al Coda

CODA

I LEFT MY HEART IN SAN FRANCISCO

Words by DOUGLASS CROSS
Music by GEORGE CORY

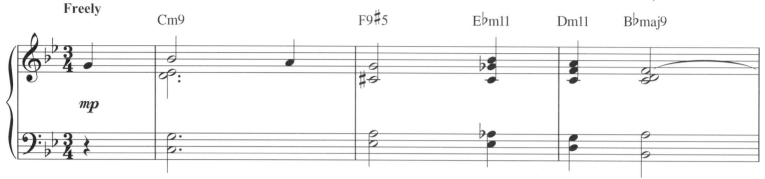

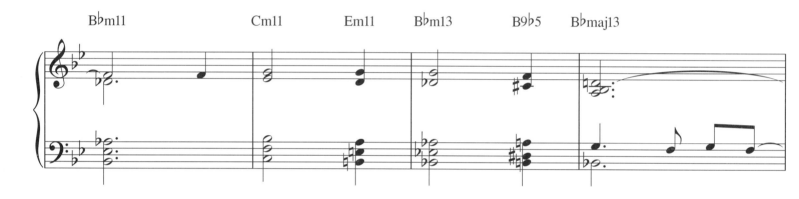

F7sus   Db/F   F7b9   Ebm/F   B/F

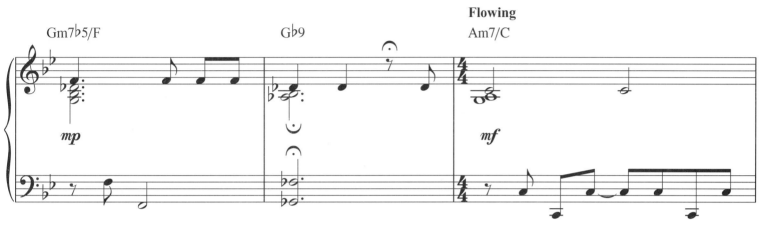

Flowing

Gm7b5/F   Gb9   Am7/C

mp   *mf*

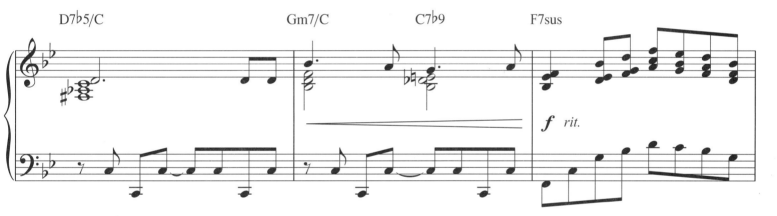

D7b5/C   Gm7/C   C7b9   F7sus

f *rit.*

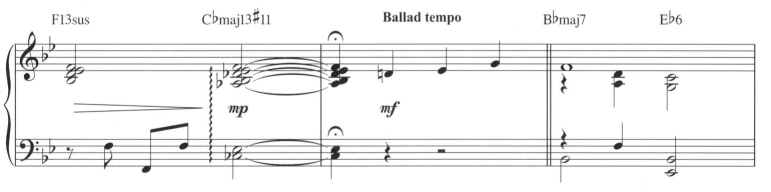

F13sus   Cbmaj13#11   **Ballad tempo**   Bbmaj7   Eb6

mp   *mf*

Dm7   C#dim7   Cm9   F9   E9   F9

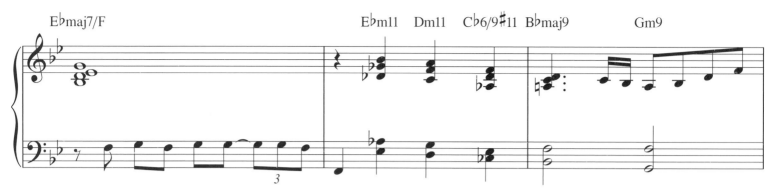

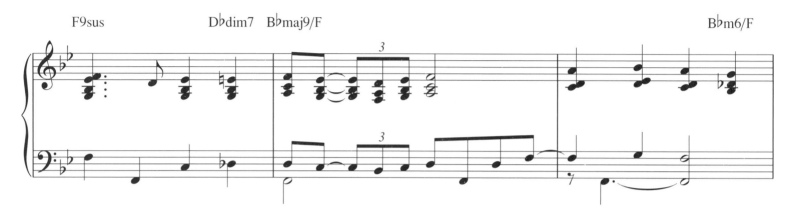

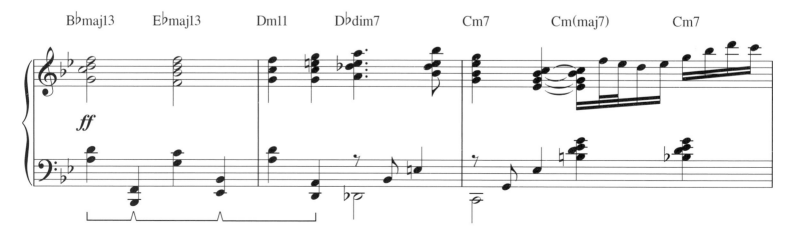

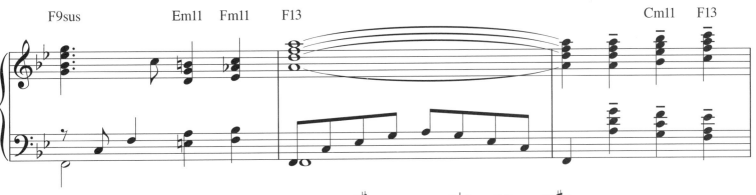

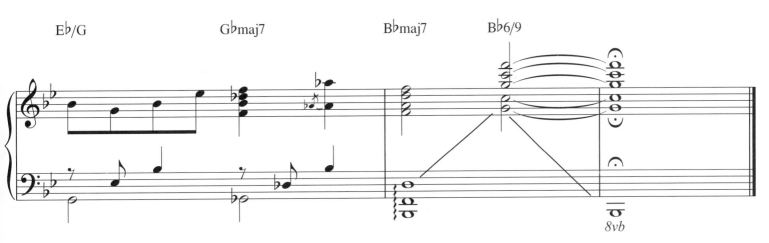

I'M IN THE MOOD FOR LOVE

Words and Music by JIMMY McHUGH
and DOROTHY FIELDS

Ballad

With pedal

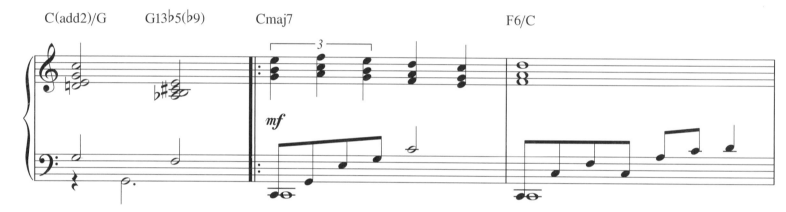

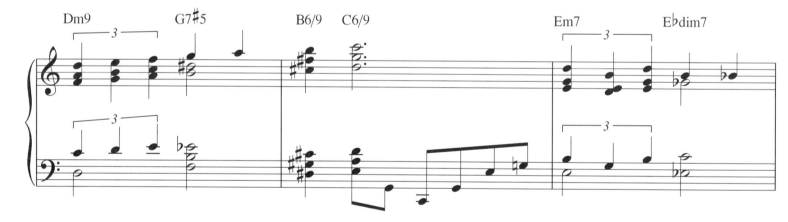

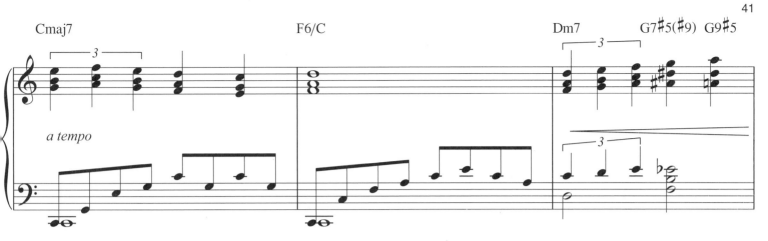

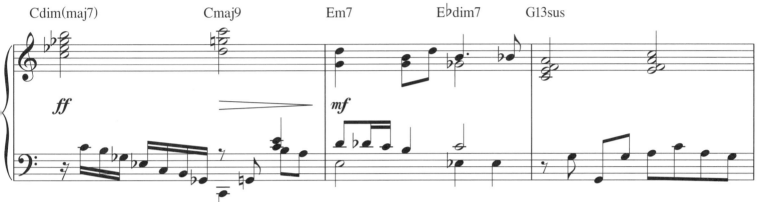

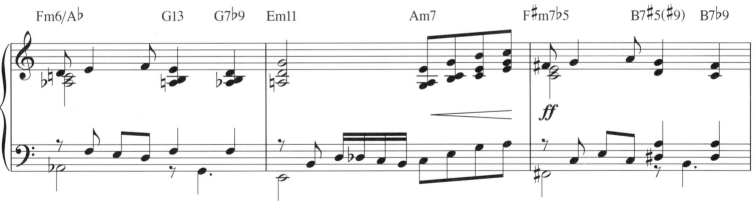

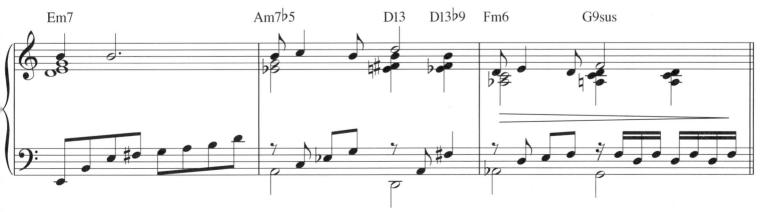

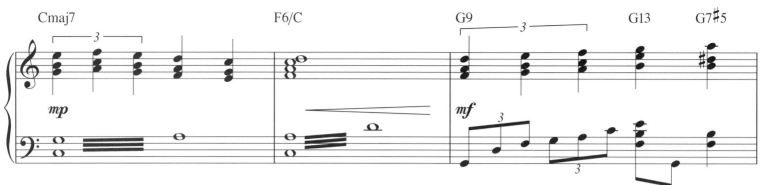

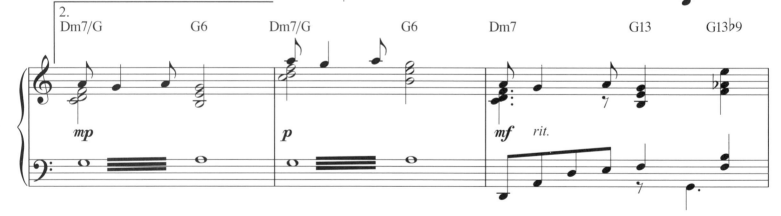

LULLABY OF BIRDLAND

Words by GEORGE DAVID WEISS
Music by GEORGE SHEARING

Moderate Swing

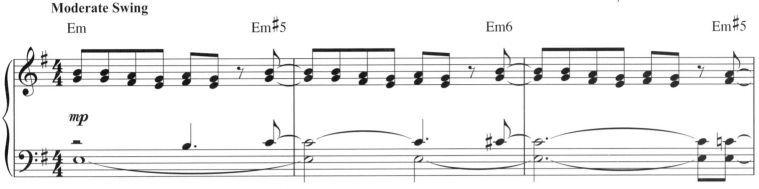

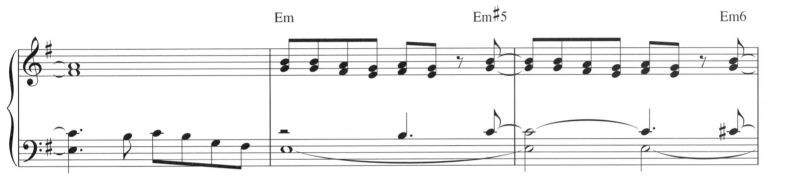

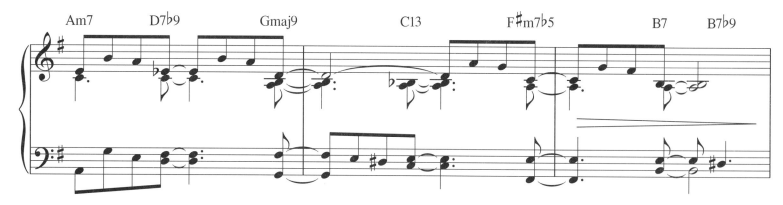

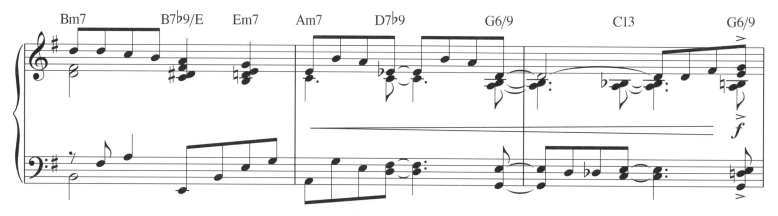

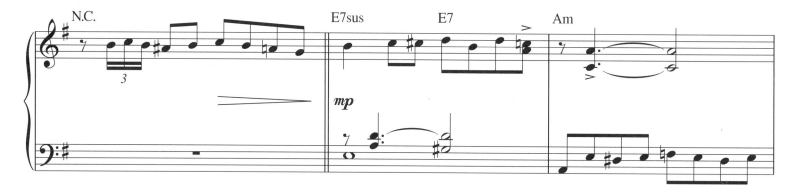

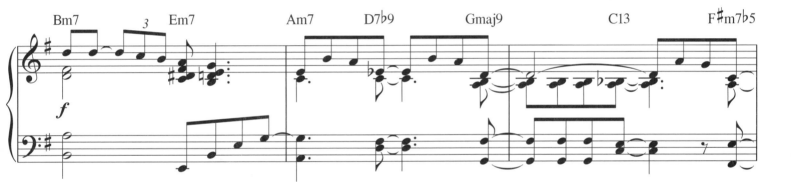

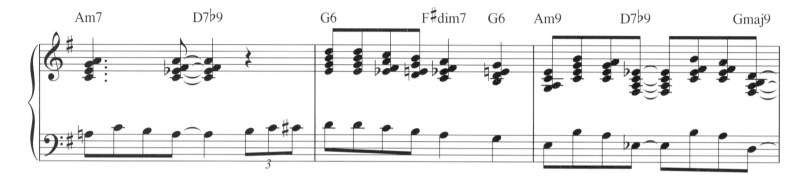

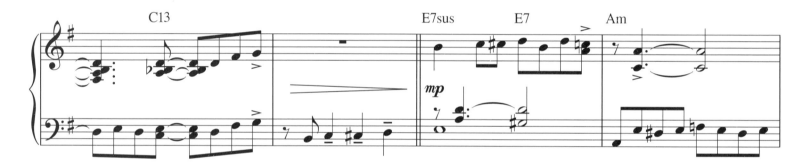

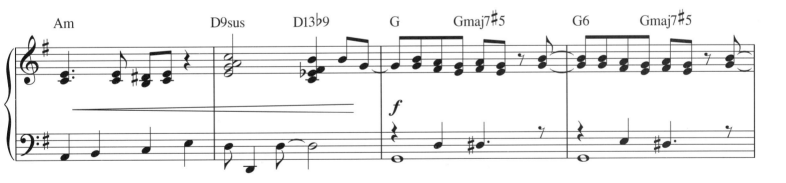

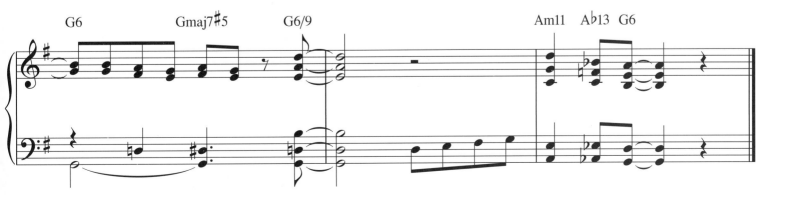

THE LADY IS A TRAMP
from BABES IN ARMS

Words by LORENZ HART
Music by RICHARD RODGERS

Moderate Swing

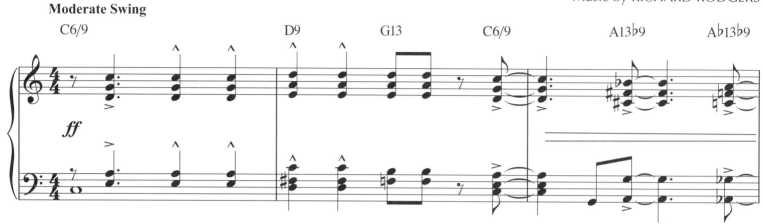

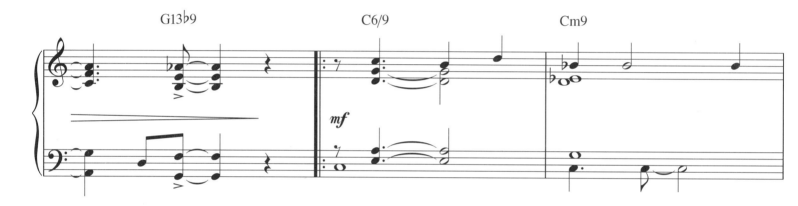

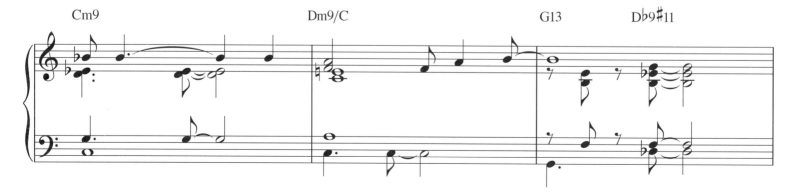

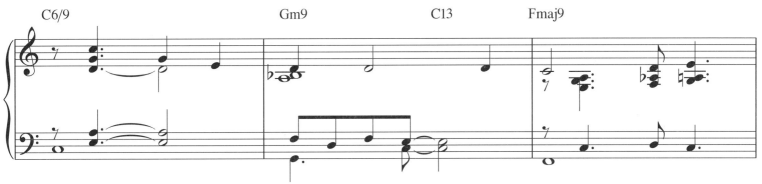

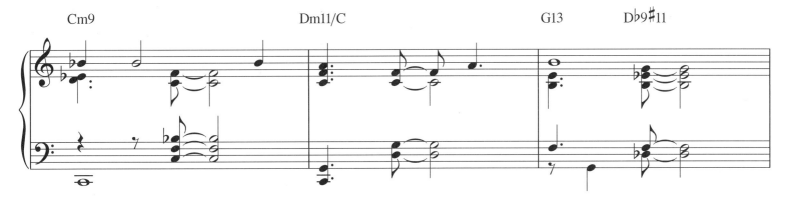

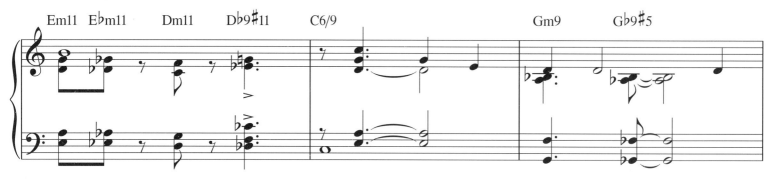

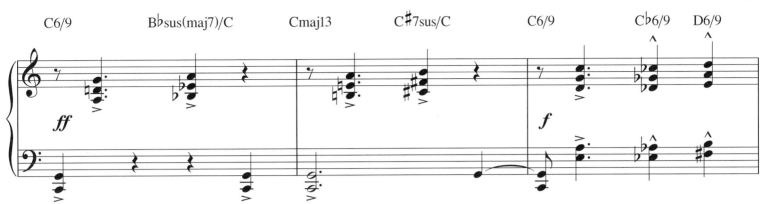

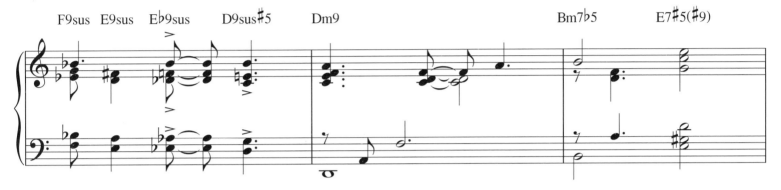

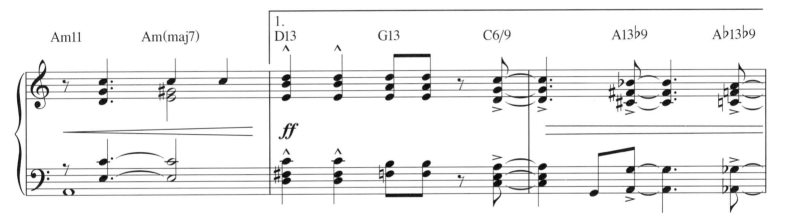

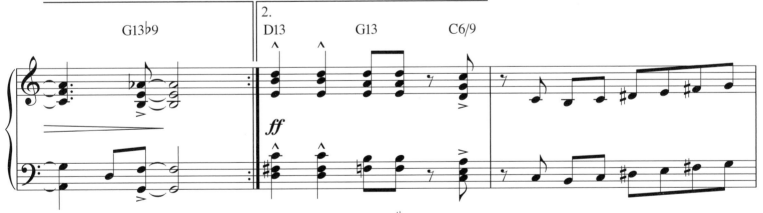

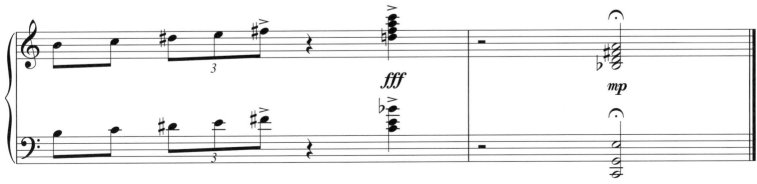

LONG AGO
(And Far Away)
from COVER GIRL

Words by IRA GERSHWIN
Music by JEROME KERN

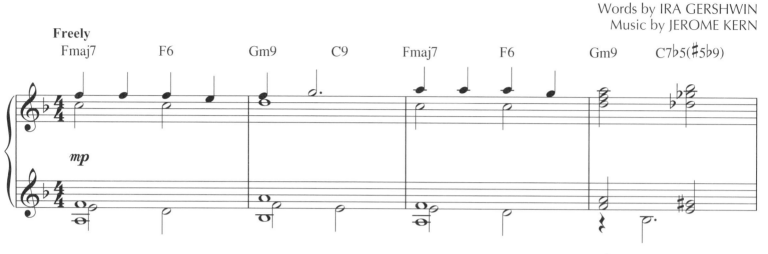

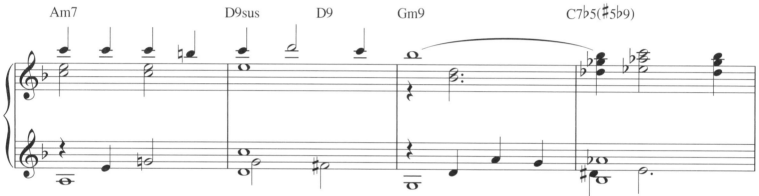

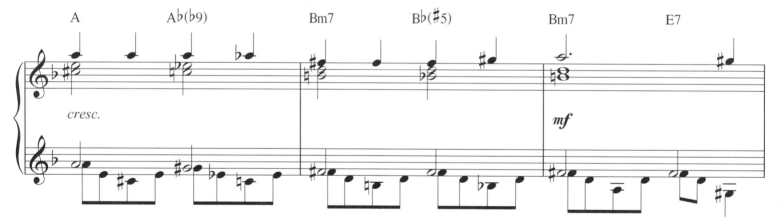

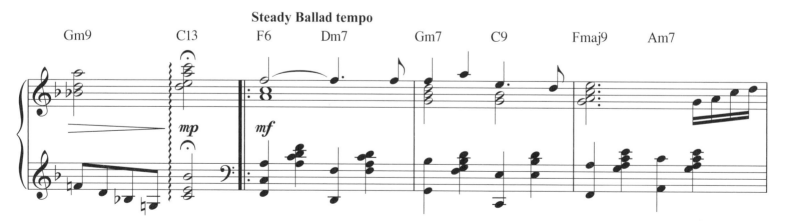

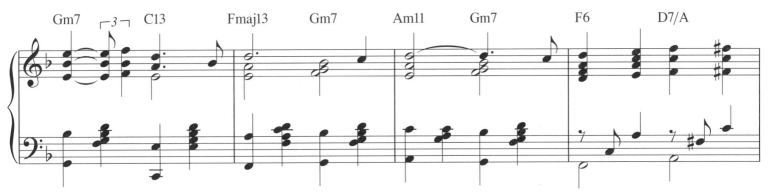

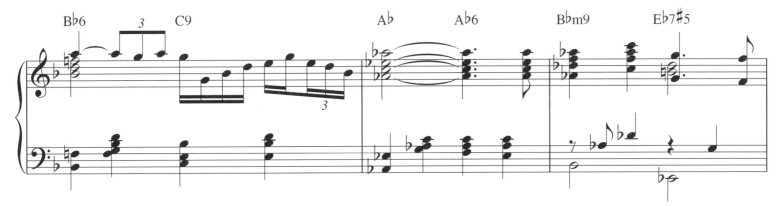

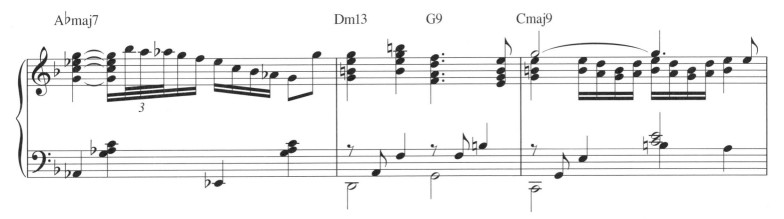

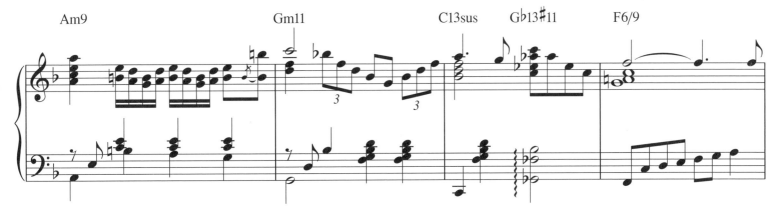

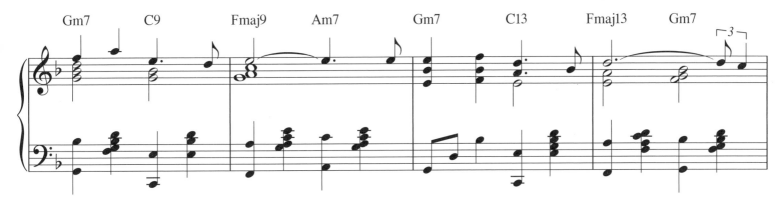

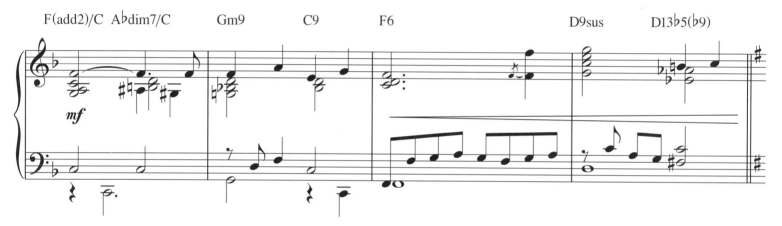

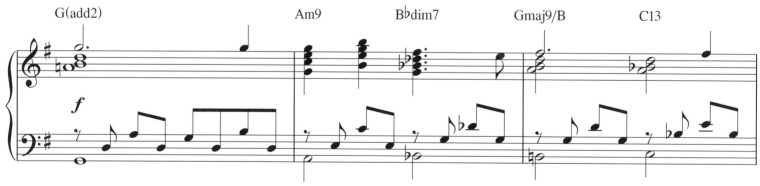

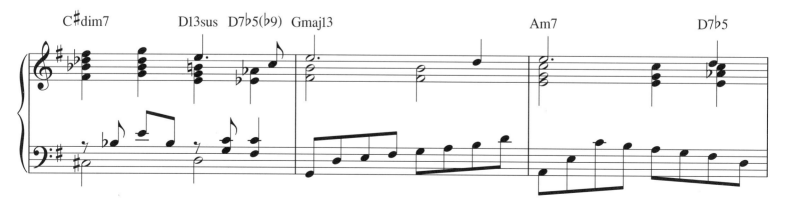

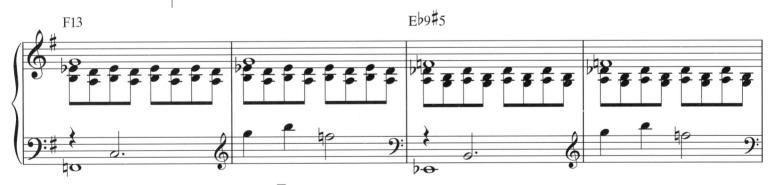

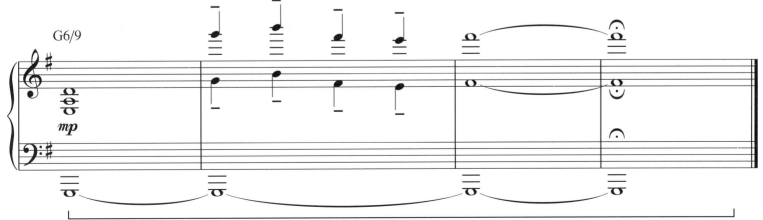

MACK THE KNIFE
from THE THREEPENNY OPERA

English Words by MARC BLITZSTEIN
Original German Words by BERT BRECHT
Music by KURT WEILL

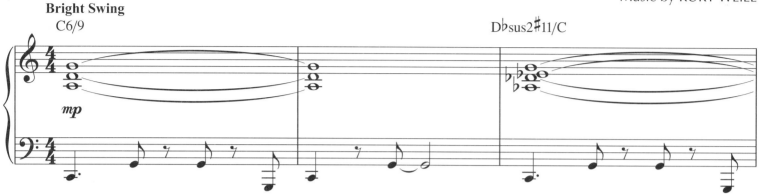

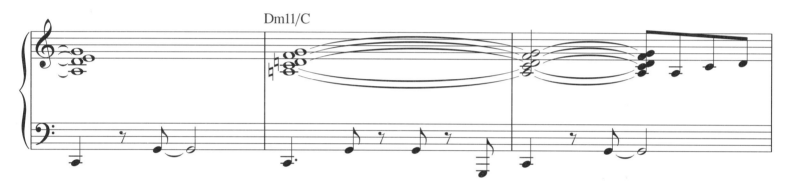

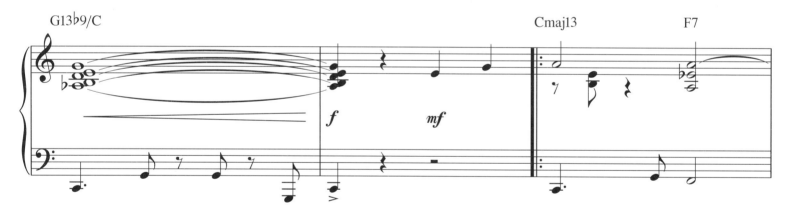

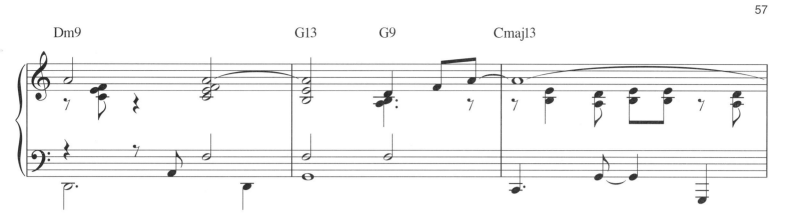

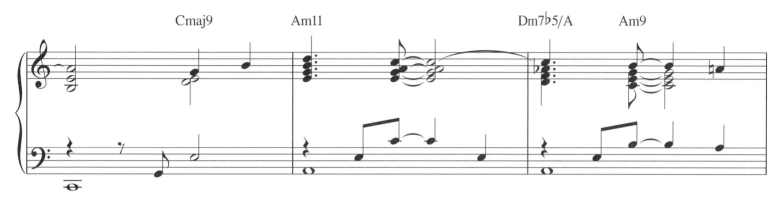

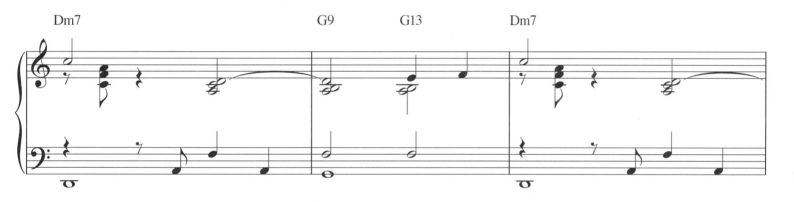

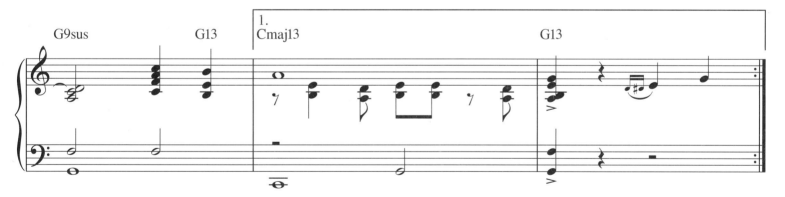

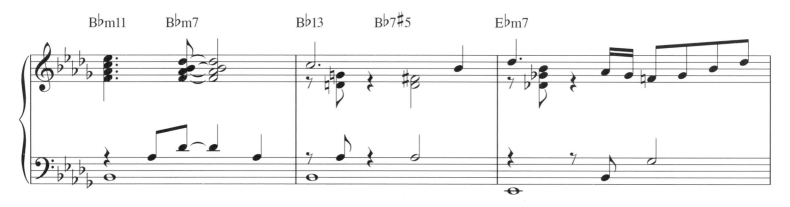

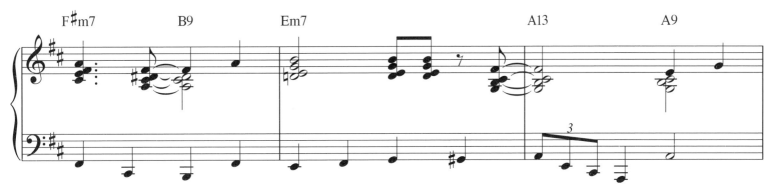

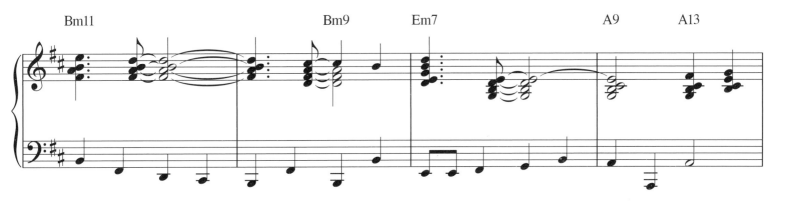

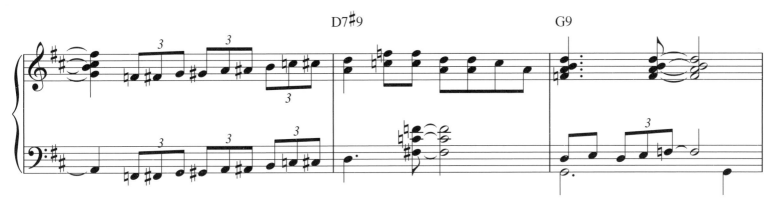

60

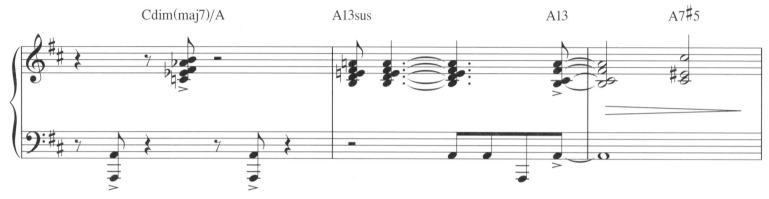

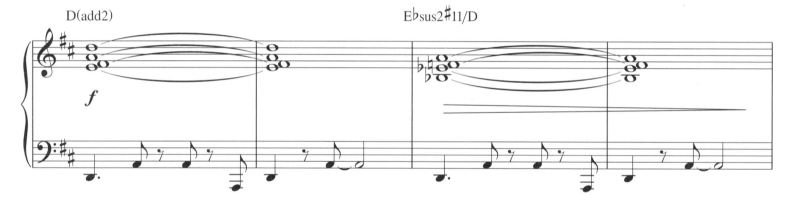

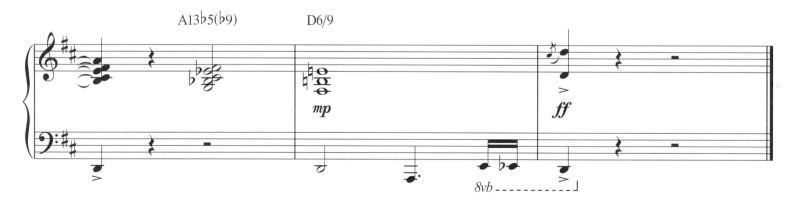

MORE
(Ti guarderò nel cuore)
from the film MONDO CANE

Music by NINO OLIVIERO and RIZ ORTOLANI
Italian Lyrics by MARCELLO CIORCIOLINI
English Lyrics by NORMAN NEWELL

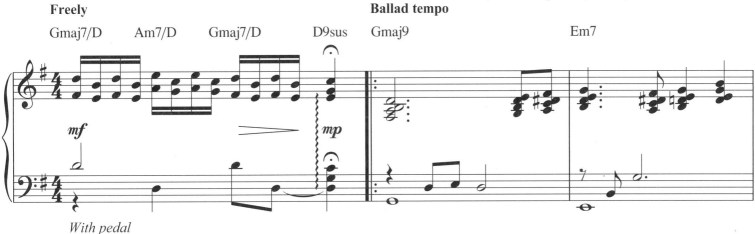

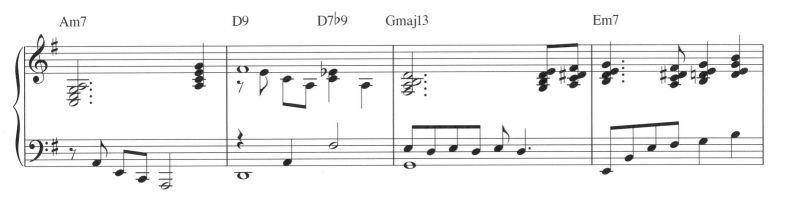

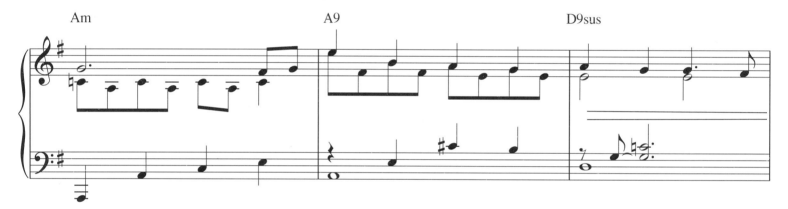

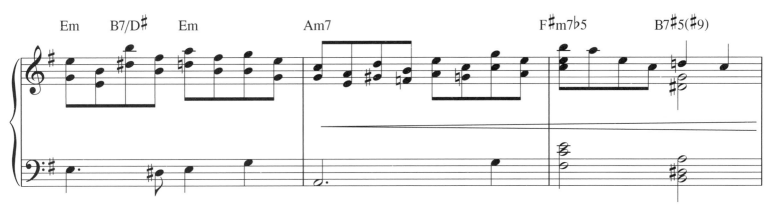

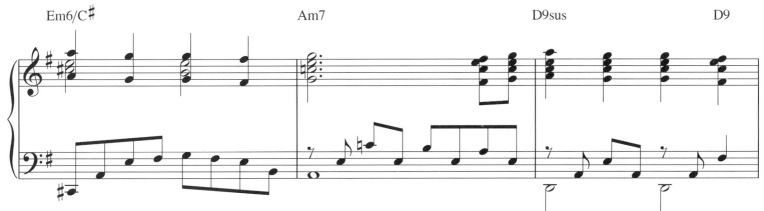

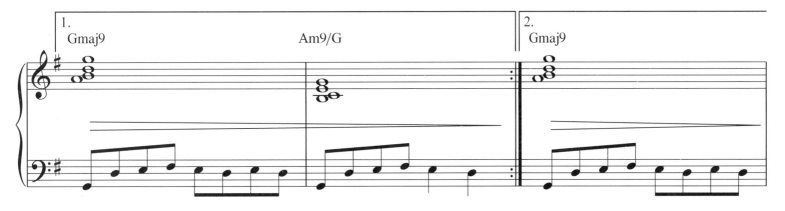

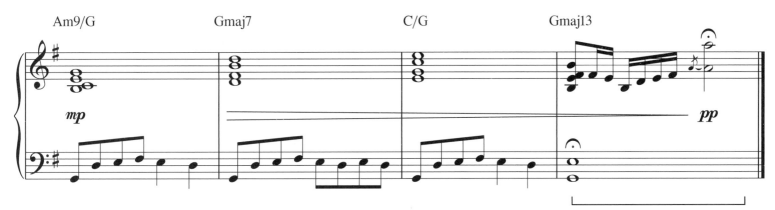

A NIGHTINGALE SANG IN BERKELEY SQUARE

Lyric by ERIC MASCHWITZ
Music by MANNING SHERWIN

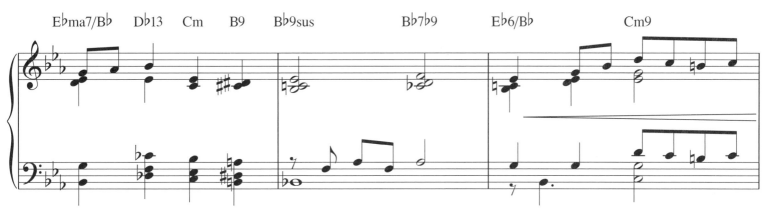

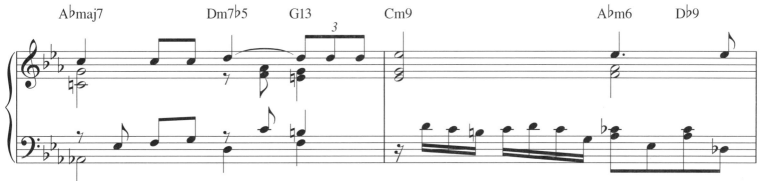

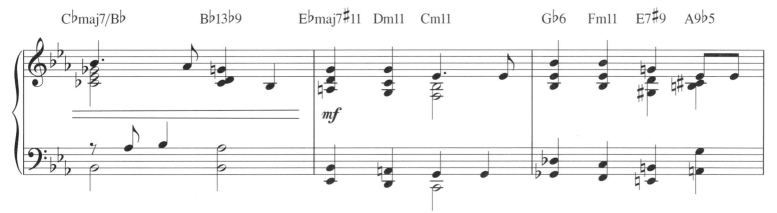

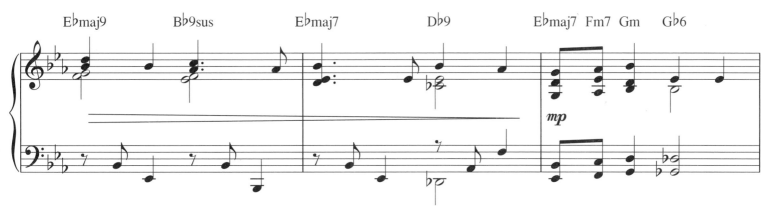

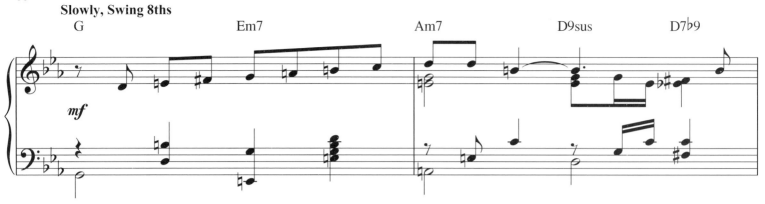

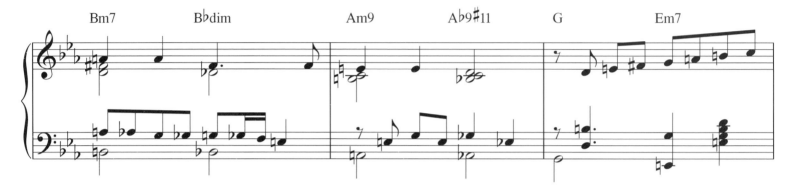

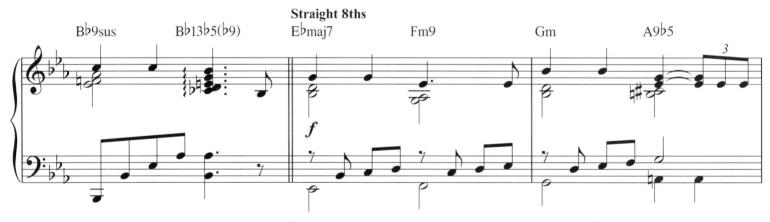

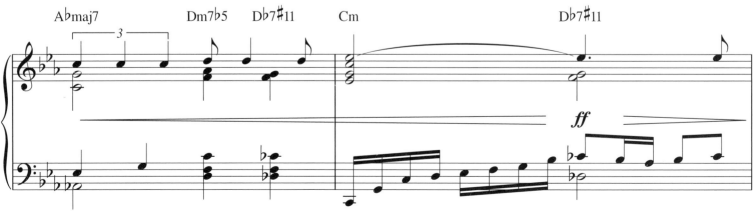

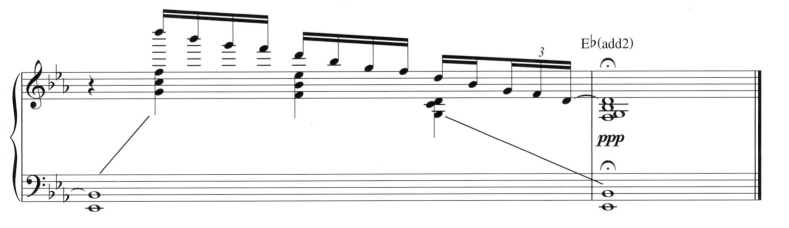

ONCE IN A WHILE

Words by BUD GREEN
Music by MICHAEL EDWARDS

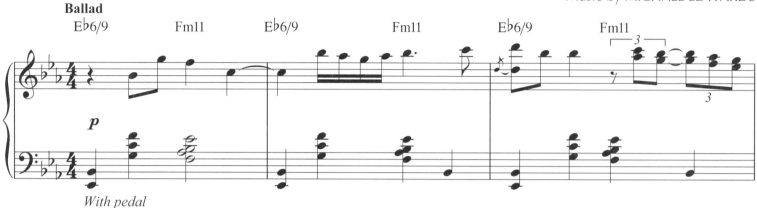

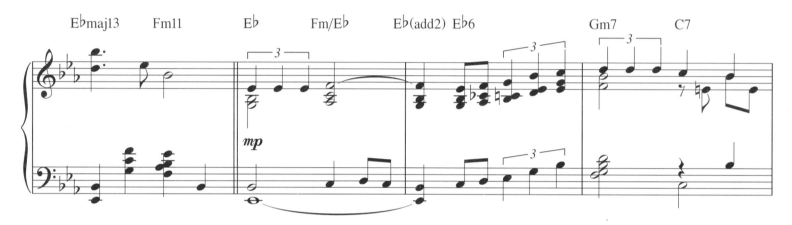

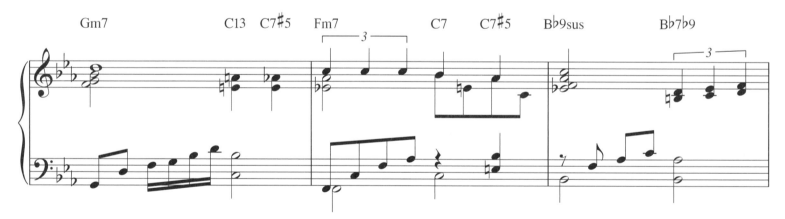

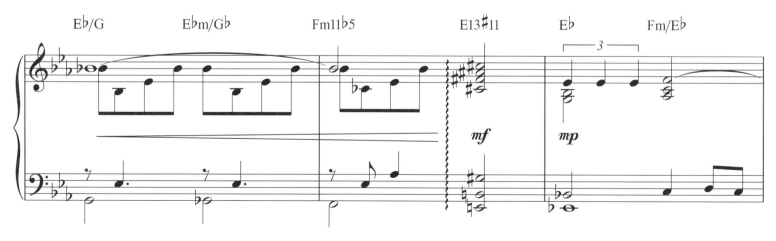

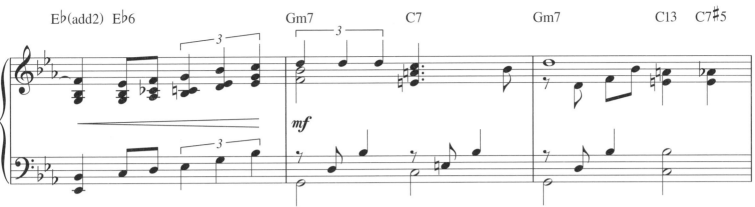

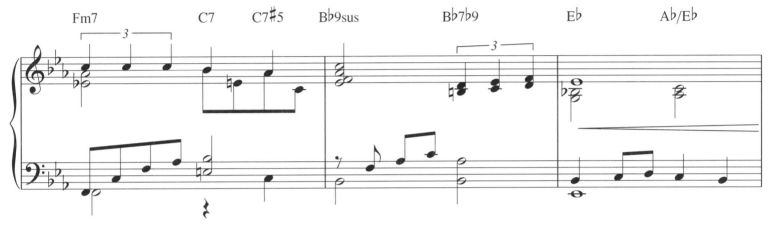

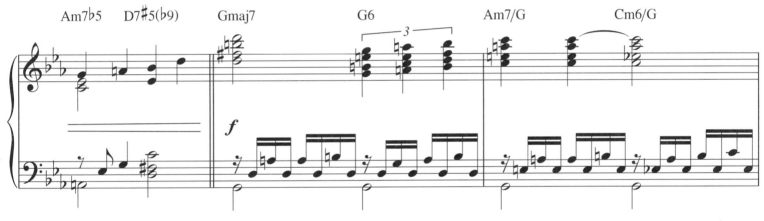

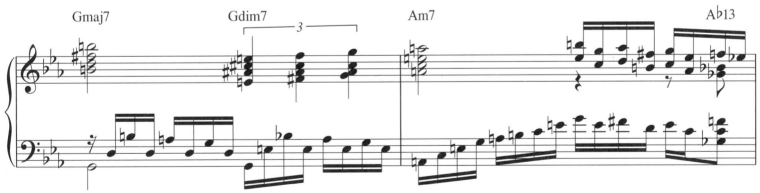

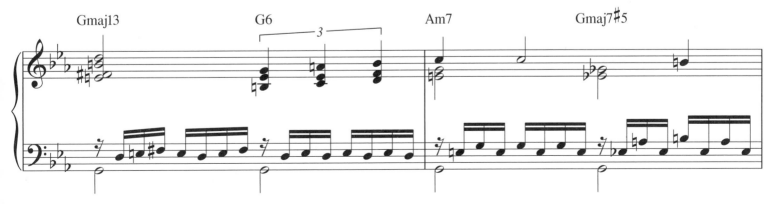

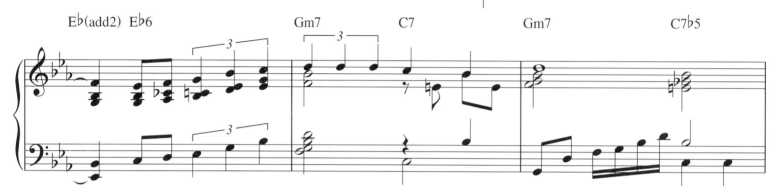

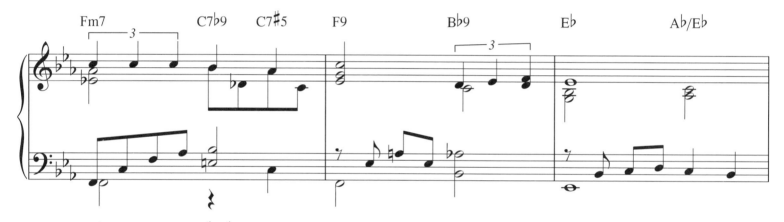

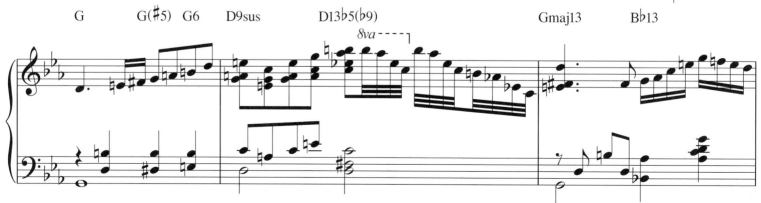

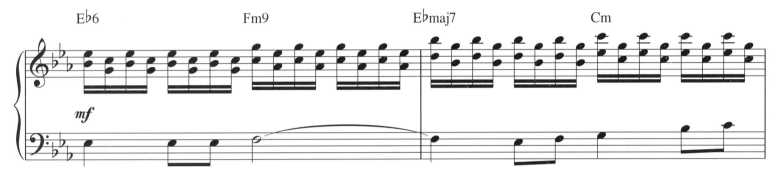

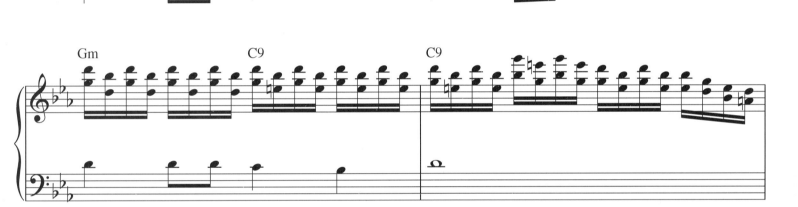

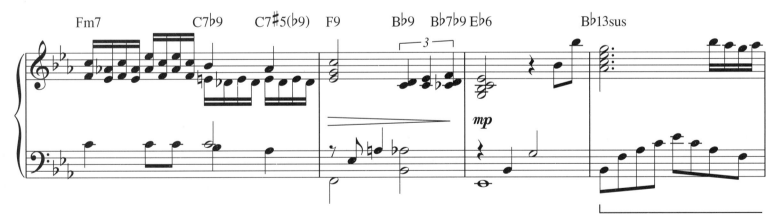

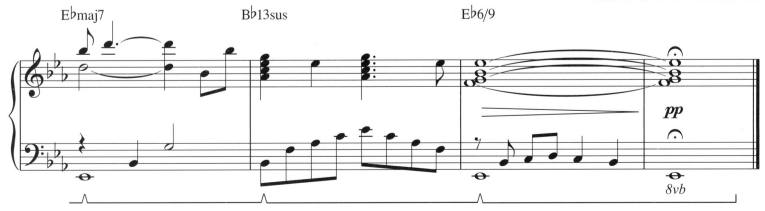

OVER THE RAINBOW

from THE WIZARD OF OZ

Music by HAROLD ARLEN
Lyric by E.Y. "YIP" HARBURG

Bright funky groove (♪♪ = ♪♪)

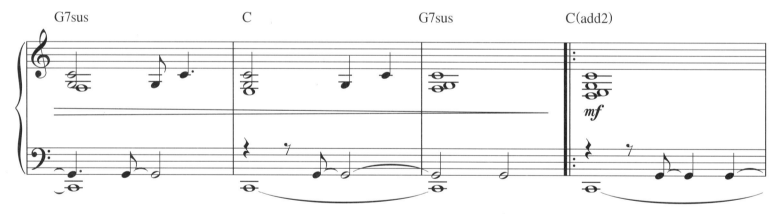

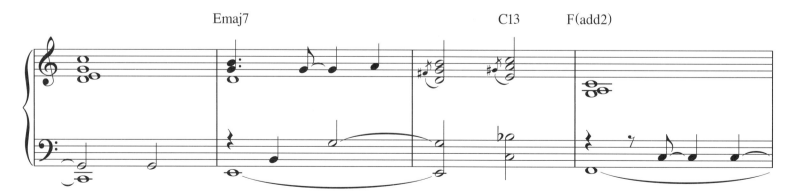

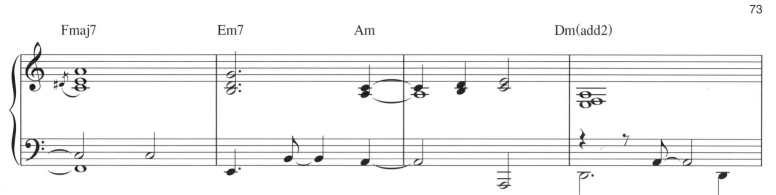

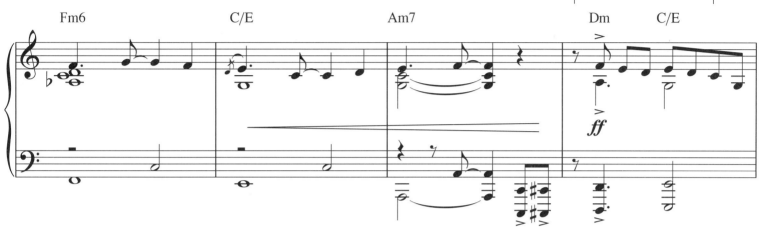

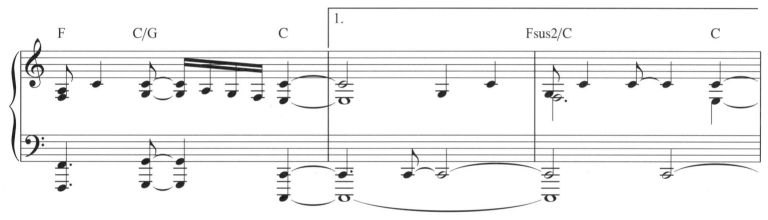

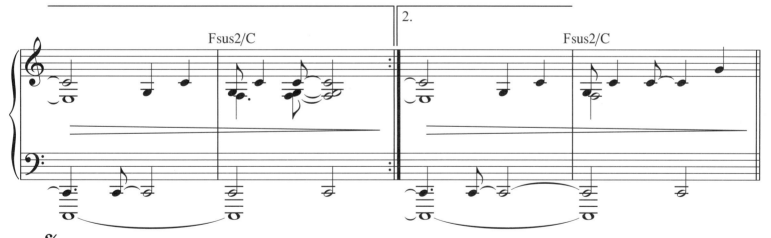

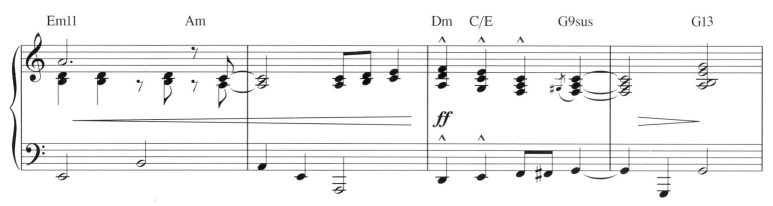

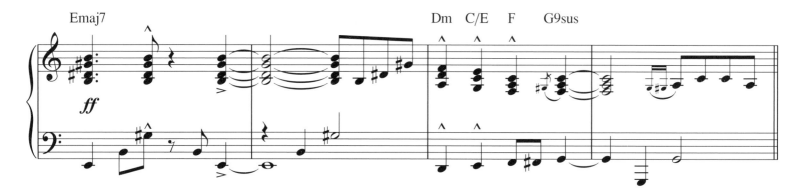

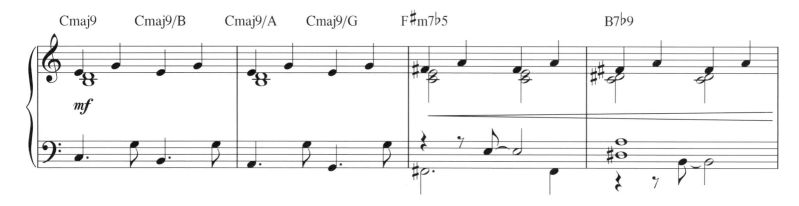

PUTTIN' ON THE RITZ

from the Motion Picture PUTTIN' ON THE RITZ

Words and Music by
IRVING BERLIN

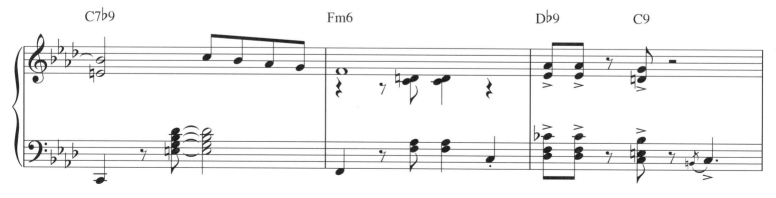

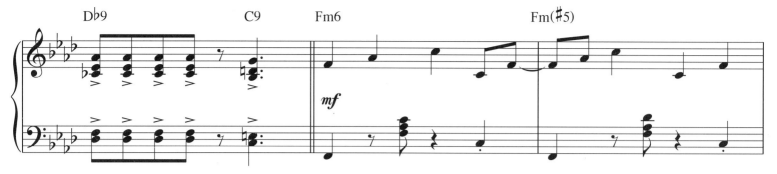

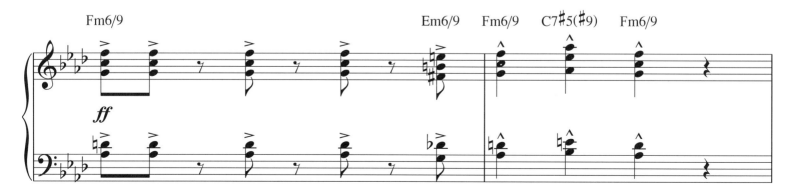

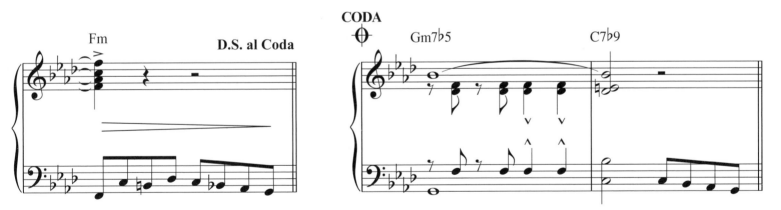

SEPTEMBER IN THE RAIN

Words by AL DUBIN
Music by HARRY WARREN

Moderate Swing

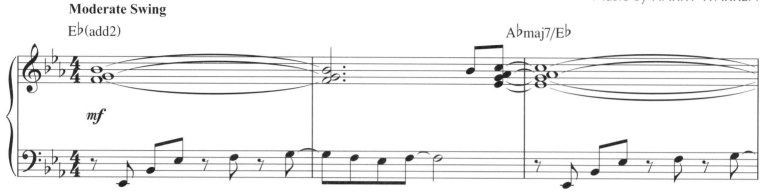

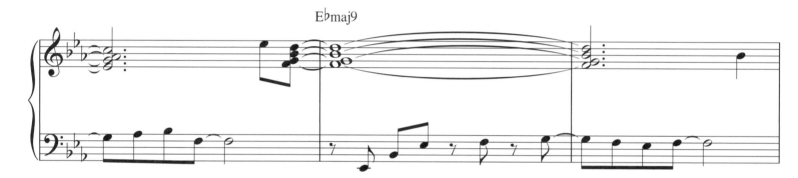

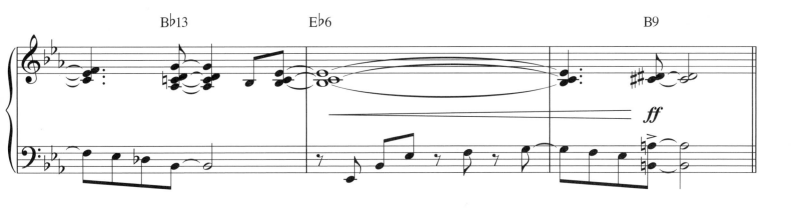

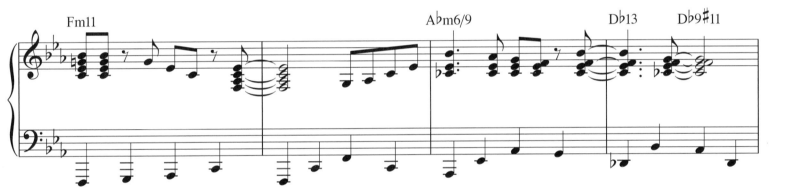

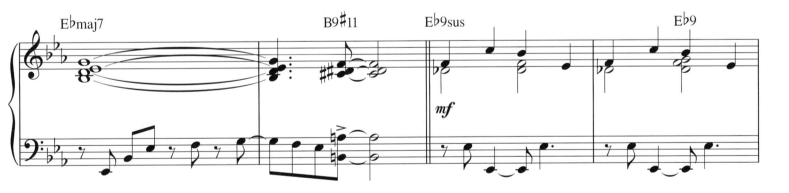

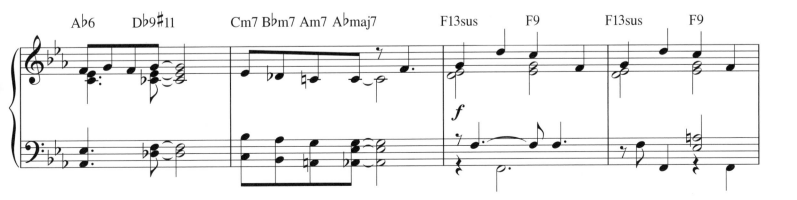

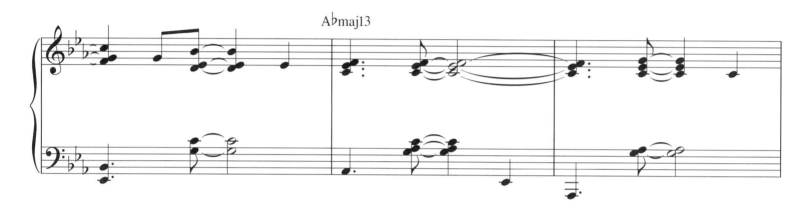

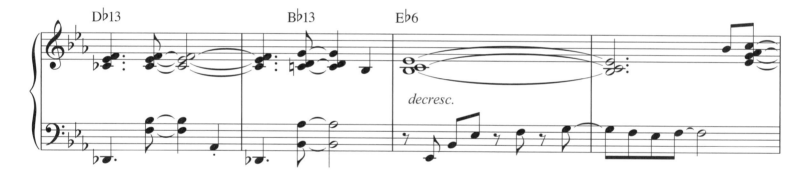

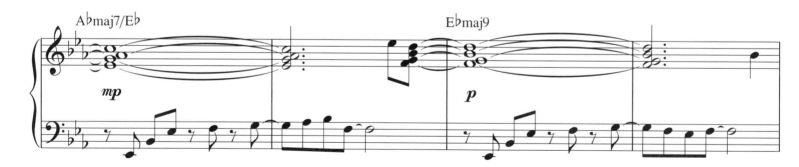

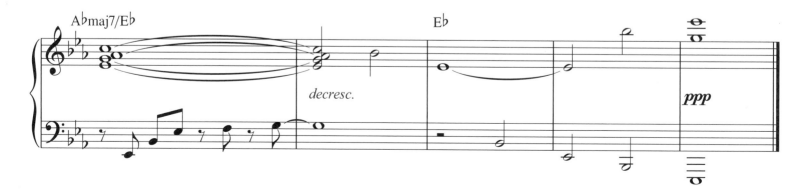

SPEAK LOW
from the Musical Production ONE TOUCH OF VENUS

Words by OGDEN NASH
Music by KURT WEILL

Moderate Latin groove

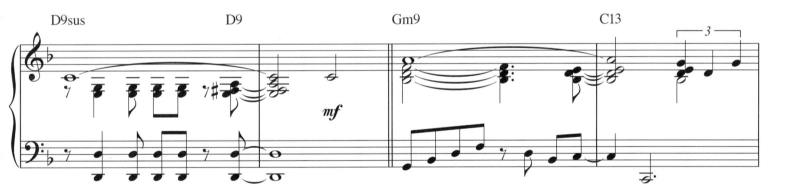

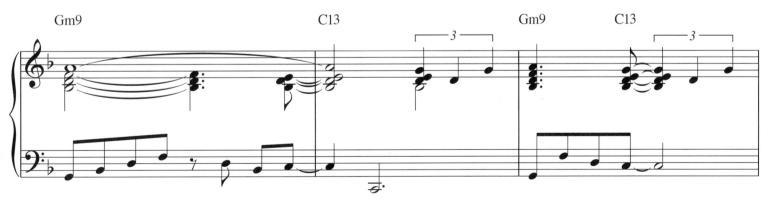

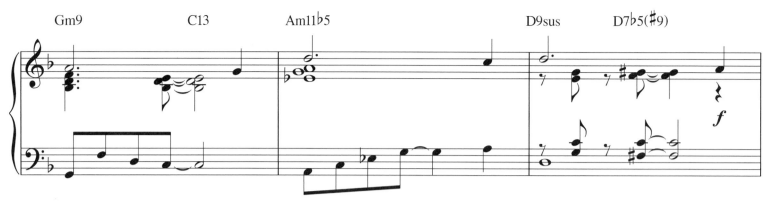

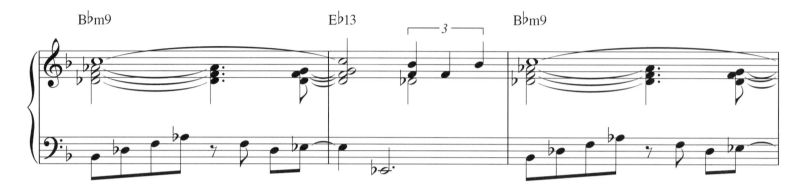

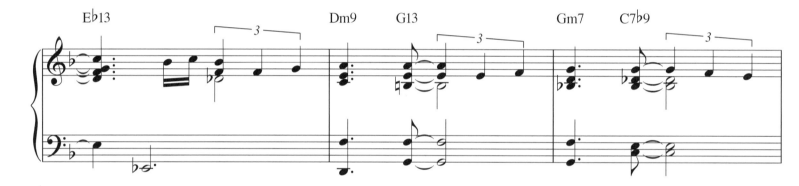

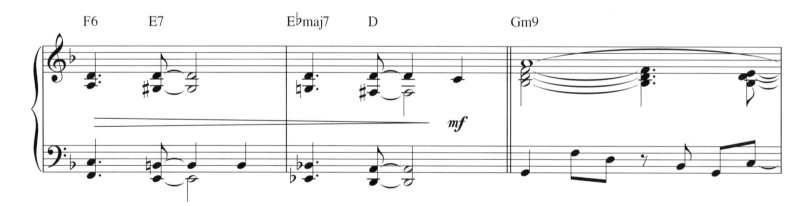

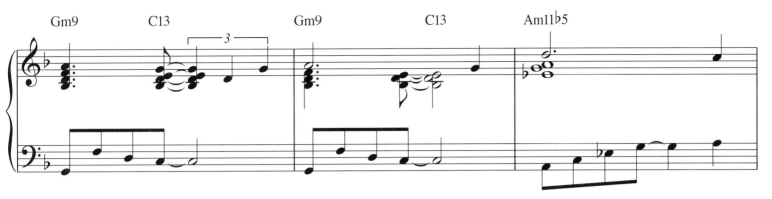

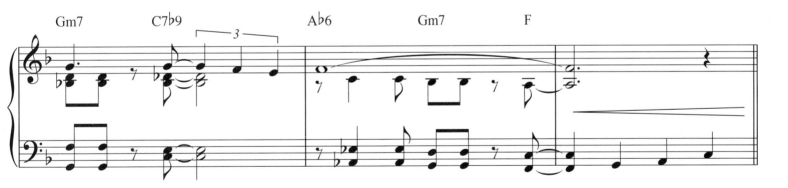

Straight 8ths

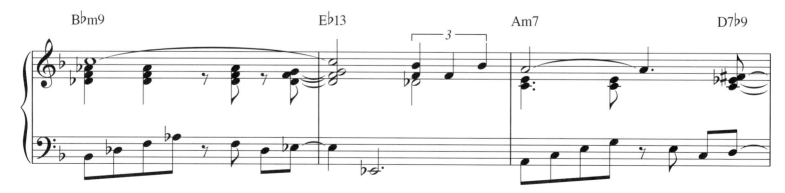

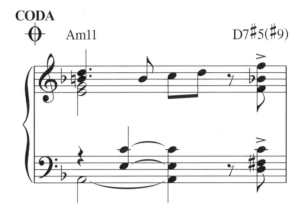

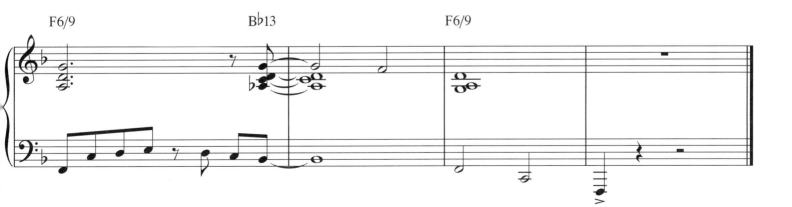

STARDUST

Music by
HOAGY CARMICHAEL

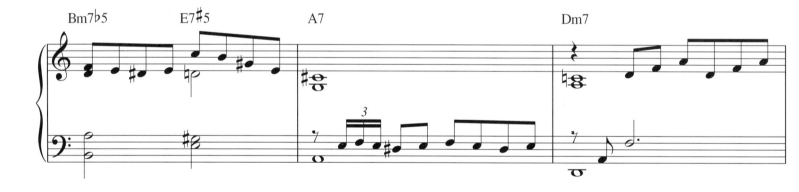

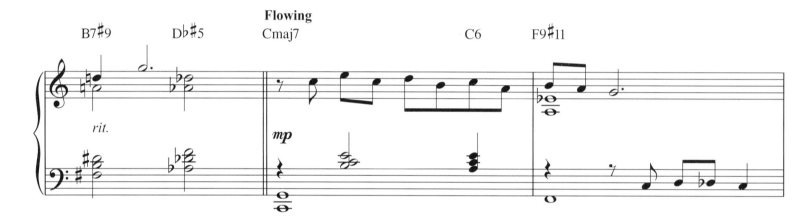

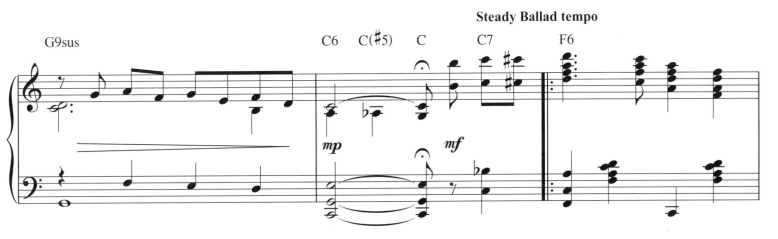

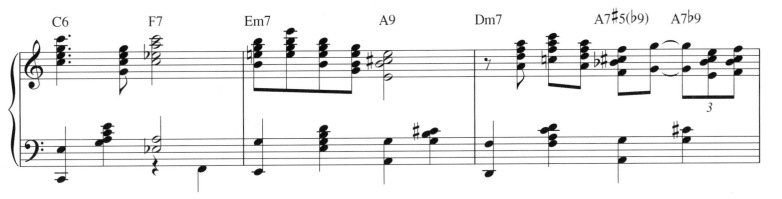

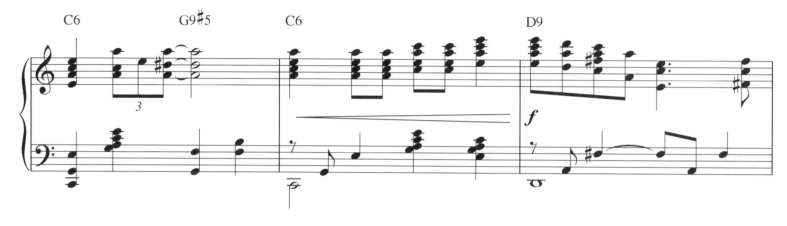

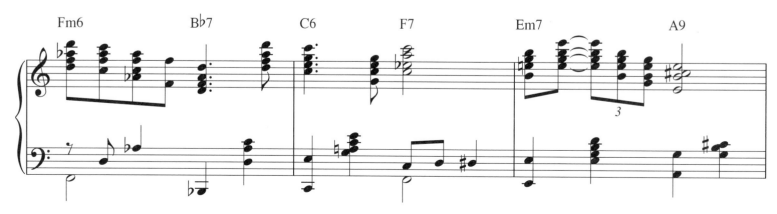

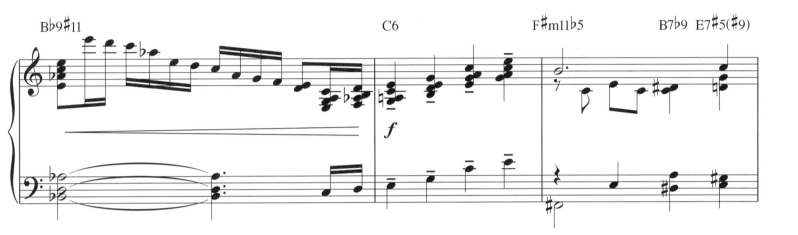

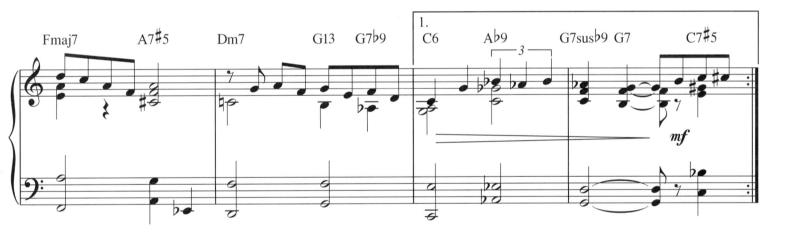

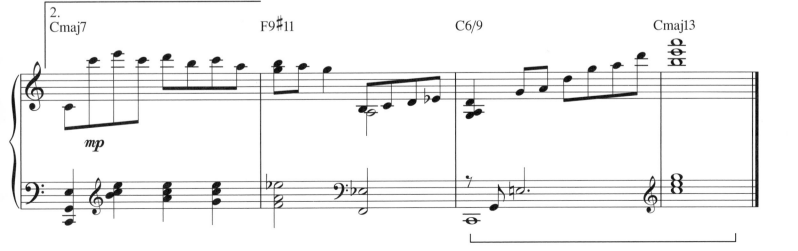

THE VERY THOUGHT OF YOU

Words and Music by
RAY NOBLE

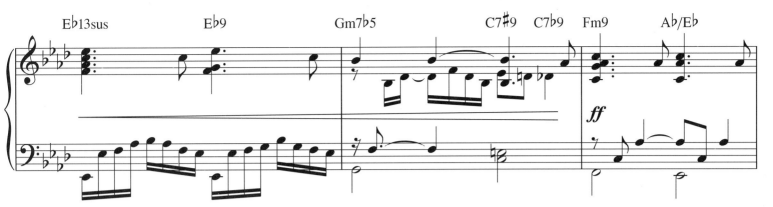

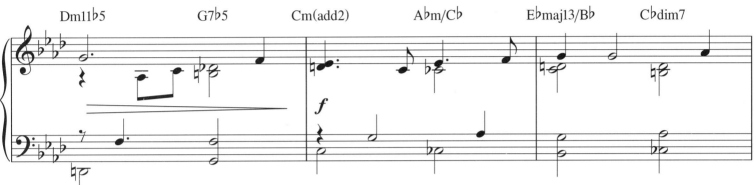

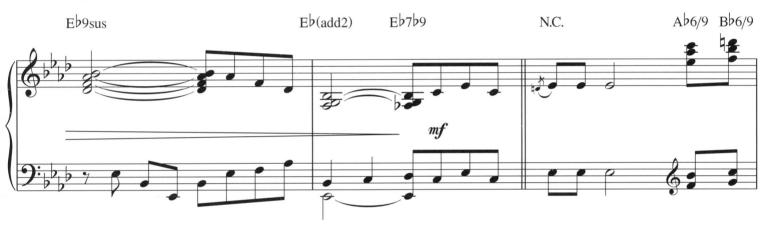

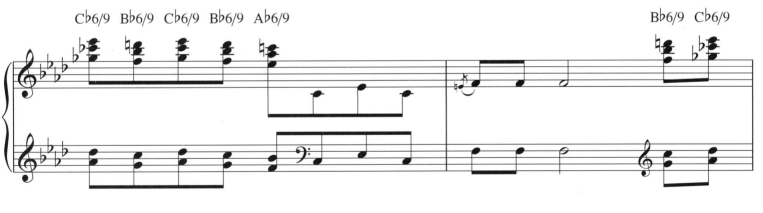

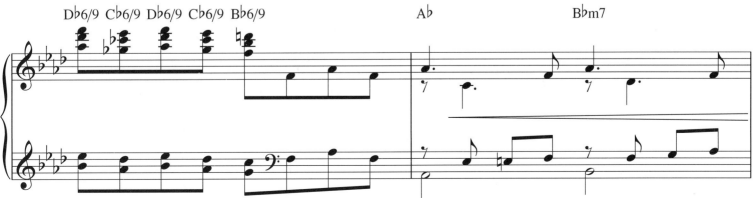

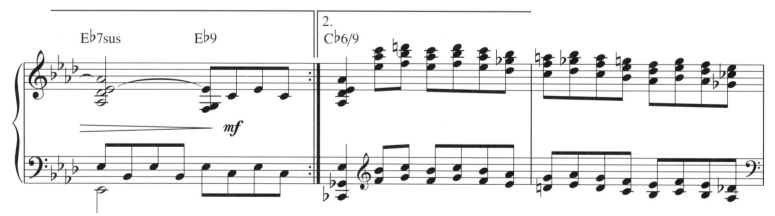

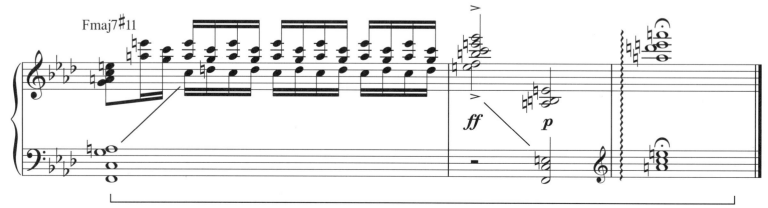